Wildlife Pest Control around Gardens and Homes

SECOND EDITION

Terrell P. Salmon
Desley A. Whisson
Rex E. Marsh

University of California
Agriculture and Natural Resources
Publication 21385

ORDERING
For information about ordering this publication, contact

University of California
Agriculture and Natural Resources
Communication Services
6701 San Pablo Avenue, 2nd Floor
Oakland, California 94608-1239

Telephone 1-800-994-8849
(510) 642-2431
FAX (510) 643-5470
E-mail: danrcs@ucdavis.edu
Visit the ANR Communication Services Web site
at http://anrcatalog.ucdavis.edu

Publication 21385

This publication has been anonymously peer reviewed for technical accuracy by University of California scientists and other qualified professionals. This review process was managed by the ANR Associate Editor for Pest Management.

ISBN-13: 978-1-879906-67-9
ISBN-10: 1-879906-67-8
Library of Congress Control Number: 2005907947

Cover: Eastern fox squirrel. Photo by Jerry P. Clark; design by Celeste Rusconi. Photo credits appear on page vi.

♻ Printed in Canada on recycled paper.

To simplify information, trade names of products have been used. No endorsement of named or illustrated products is intended, nor is criticism implied of similar products that are not mentioned or illustrated.

4.5m-pr-12/05-SB/CR

Contents

Acknowledgments

We would like to express our special thanks to Stephen Barnett for his editing and technical assistance. Thanks also go to Robert E. Lickliter, the coauthor of the previous edition of this book, for we drew heavily from the information he helped assemble and write. To all who contributed photographs for inclusion, we cannot thank you enough. A thank you also to Paul Gorenzel for his assistance in assembling the photographs. Finally, our gratitude is extended to the anonymous peer reviewers.

Photo Credits

Tracy Borland: fig. 81. **Dell O. Clark:** figs. 5, 12, 14. **Jack Kelly Clark:** figs. 53, 85, 91. **Jerry P. Clark:** figs. 2, 4, 6, 7, 8, 9, 10, 11, 13, 19, 48, 50, 51, 55, 61, 62, 63, 64, 68, 70, 87, 100, 109, 110, 116, 126, 130, 131, 132. **W. Paul Gorenzel:** figs. 3, 15, 16, 27, 28, 30, 37, 38, 41, 43, 52, 71, 101. **Rex E. Marsh:** figs. 35, 49, 58, 60, 73, 75, 76, 80, 83, 92, 93, 95, 98, 113, 114, 118, 137, 138. **Ron Mumme:** fig. 33. **Ross O'Connell:** figs. 78, 90, 102. **Terrell P. Salmon:** figs. 42, 44, 65, 66, 84, 96, 97, 99, 119. **Allen Tunberg:** figs. 67, 112.

About the Authors

Terrell P. Salmon is a wildlife specialist for the University of California Cooperative Extension. His career has encompassed every aspect of wildlife pest control in California, and his research interests include the ecology, behavior, population dynamics, and control of vertebrates with particular emphasis on those affecting agricultural production and public health. He is the author of several pest notes on wildlife, as well as other publications protecting California agriculture from vertebrate pests.

Desley A. Whisson is a former University of California Cooperative Extension Wildlife Specialist at the University of California, Davis. Her research interests include population ecology of small mammals, management of exotic vertebrates (roof rats and mongooses) for native species conservation, habitat modification for wildlife damage management, indexing techniques for vertebrates, and reduced-risk baiting strategies for rodent control. She is currently a researcher with the Department of Environment and Heritage, South Australia.

Rex E. Marsh is an emeritus specialist in vertebrate ecology in the Department of Wildlife, Fish, and Conservation Biology at the University of California, Davis. His research interests include ecology, vertebrate behavior, and management and control of wild vertebrates, and he is a foremost expert on rodent control. He has published extensively on wildlife and vertebrate pest control.

Wildlife Pests

WILDLIFE PESTS are often defined as free-living vertebrates that adversely affect the health or well-being of people or conflict in some other way with human activities. Some wildlife are considered pests because they are implicated in the transmission of diseases to people (table 1). Certain wildlife may be pests in one situation but highly desirable in other situations. It is the activity, not the species, that defines the pest.

WHY WILDLIFE BECOME PESTS

Wildlife that become pests are almost always those that have little fear of living close to humans and their dwellings. These areas usually provide an array of highly desirable food. Typically, home and garden areas provide ornamentals, vegetables, and fruit and nut trees. We fertilize and irrigate the garden and turf, promoting luxurious growth during the drier summer months, which only adds to the attraction for certain wildlife. Food and water for pets and domestic animals often provide further wildlife food resources. Sometimes we deliberately feed wildlife. We should not be surprised that, as a result of these and other activities, conflicts between wildlife and people are common.

In many situations, wildlife populations cycle according to weather and other factors. Some species, such as meadow voles, become a significant pest in the home garden only during a high point in a cycle when they become very numerous. Some animals, such as deer or pocket gophers, can be a problem when only one or two are present in a garden.

TOLERANCE OF WILDLIFE PROBLEMS

Some people like to see wildlife nearby and choose to accept a certain amount of damage rather than attempt to eliminate the pest or deprive them of the food or shelter they seek. For some wildlife in certain situations, tolerating them is about the only option, since an attempt to manage or control them is neither practical nor feasible. The introduced Eastern fox squirrel is a good example because it may be so numerous throughout a neighborhood that controlling it in your garden will have no lasting impact. Deer, opossums, and raccoons also present limited management approaches. Homeowners must often take whatever practical action they can to minimize the problem and then accept the occasional visitors.

INTEGRATED PEST MANAGEMENT

The information provided in this volume is in keeping with the principles of integrated pest management (IPM) and offers the widest range possible of both preventive (indirect control) and population reduction (direct control) methods. IPM is an ecological approach to managing wildlife pests and usually involves the use of two or more management methods or techniques encompassing exclusion, sanitation, modification of habitats, trapping, chemical repellents, frightening devices, shooting, and the selective use of appropriate toxic pesticides such as baits or burrow fumigants. In selecting toxic pesticides, environmental protection and the safety of the public

Trapping Laws and Regulations

In 1998, California voters passed Proposition 4, the Wildlife Body-Gripping Traps Ban, Animal Poison Initiative, which prohibits the use of body-gripping traps to capture wildlife for recreational or commercial purposes. In most cases, traps used for animals causing damage around homes and gardens are not considered body-gripping traps. These include cage and box traps, nets, and common rat and mouse traps. Exceptions appear to be some pocket gopher traps and the Conibear trap, which is used for squirrels and rats. However, these traps can be used when animals are causing or threatening to cause problems around your home or garden as long as that is the sole purpose of the trapping effort. The use of steel-jawed leghold traps is not allowed.

and nontarget animals are of the utmost importance, with an emphasis on reducing overall pesticide use. Early pest detection accompanied by quick action dramatically limits the amount of pesticide needed.

Important components of IPM are the proper identification of the pest causing the damage and the constant

appraisal of the management methods or control strategies put into place to assure that the desired results are being achieved. Once the objective has been achieved, monitoring provides an early detection of any recurrence of the wildlife problem. For more information on integrated pest management, see *IPM in Practice: Principles and*

TABLE 1.

Common human diseases and their vertebrate pest hosts

DISEASE	CAUSATIVE ORGANISM	TYPE OF ORGANISM	WILDLIFE CARRIERS
baylisascaris larval migrans	*Baylisascaris procyonis*	roundworm	raccoons
hantavirus	family Bunyaviridae	virus	deer mice, other native rodents
histoplasmosis	*Histoplasma capsulatum*	fungus	bats (droppings), birds
LCM	lymphocytic choriomeningitis virus	virus	house mice, rats, skunks
leptospirosis	*Leptospira interrogans*	bacteria	mice, rats, skunks
listeriosis	*Listeria monocytogenes*	bacteria	skunks
Lyme disease	*Borrelia burgdorferi*	bacteria	deer mice (white-footed mice), deer
murine typhus	*Rickettsia typhi*	bacteria	rats, native rodents
plague	*Yersinia pestis*	bacteria	ground squirrels, meadow voles, rats, wood rats,
psittacosis	*Chlamydiosis psittaci*	bacteria	birds
Q fever	*Coxiella burnetti*	bacteria	rabbits, opossums, rodents
rabies	lyssavirus	virus	bats, coyotes, foxes, raccoons, skunks
rat-bite fever	*Streptobacillus* spp.	bacteria	rats, native rodents
Rocky Mountain Spotted fever	*Rickettsia rickettsii*	bacteria	opossums, rabbits, rodents
salmonellosis	*Salmonella* spp.	bacteria	birds, opossums, rodents,
toxoplasmosis	*Toxoplasma* spp.	protozoan	birds, foxes,
tularemia	*Francisella tularensis*	bacteria	rabbits, rodents

Methods of Integrated Pest Management (Flint 2001).

LEGAL CONSIDERATIONS

Applicable sections of the California Fish and Game Code and the U.S. Federal Code of Regulations protect most mammals and birds. An owner or tenant may, however, control certain wildlife species that damage growing crops or other property. A hunting license is not usually required when taking animals under this situation.

Common home and garden wildlife pests that can be controlled without special permission include

- Norway and roof rats
- house mice
- pocket gophers
- ground squirrels
- meadow voles (meadow mice)
- jackrabbits
- fox squirrels
- English sparrows (house sparrows)
- starlings
- skunks
- opossums
- raccoons

Special provisions of the California Fish and Game code must be met if traps are used; these provisions will be discussed in relation to individual wildlife species throughout this book. Some types of traps may not be legal to use. Local restrictions on controlling some animals and on using certain devices and methods do exist. Check with your local fish and game or county agricultural commissioner's office for any restrictions that may apply in your area.

CONTROLLING WILDLIFE DAMAGE

The primary objective of a wildlife control program should be to reduce damage in a practical and environmentally acceptable manner. If you base control methods on knowledge of the habits and biology of the wildlife that are causing damage, your efforts will be more effective and will serve to maximize the safety of the environment, people, and other animals.

Living with Wildlife

- ☐ Take measures to screen off spaces in which wild animals may nest or den, including chimneys.

- ☐ Do not leave pet food outdoors overnight.

- ☐ Place garbage in a container (preferably metal) that has a tight-fitting lid.

- ☐ Avoid putting food scraps in a compost pile; if you must add scraps, use a fully enclosed compost container that excludes animals.

- ☐ If you feed birds, suspend feeders at least 6 feet (1.8 m) above the ground. Mammal-proof feeders if possible.

- ☐ If you provide food for wildlife they become less self-reliant and learn to depend on people.

- ☐ Pick up and dispose of fallen fruits and nuts frequently.

- ☐ Fence, screen off, or net crops to be protected from wildlife.

- ☐ Unsecured pet entrances to a residence may provide access for wildlife such as raccoons, especially at night.

- ☐ Clean barbecue grills following use or cover them to deny animals access to food residues.

- ☐ In some areas, pets left outdoors overnight may risk encounters with wildlife that may result in injury or death.

Euthanizing Live-trapped Animals

While it is generally rec-ommended that animals should not be trapped in devices that capture them alive, some prefer live trapping, and in some situations it may be more successful. Since releasing trapped animals into new areas is prohibited by Califor-nia Fish and Game regu-lations and is generally considered to be eco-logically inappropriate, trapped animals must be euthanized humane-ly. A simple carbon dioxide (CO_2) chamber, consisting of a canister of CO_2 and a gas-tight enclosure, can be used. Because CO_2 is heavier than air, it will flow into a chamber and remain there as long the cham-ber is closed. To use a CO_2 chamber, place the trap containing the live animal in the chamber and fill it with CO_2. Seal the chamber and wait about 5 minutes. Dis-pose of the animal as illustrated in figure 1.

A key to controlling wildlife damage is prompt and accurate identification of the wildlife species causing the damage. This book deals with common wildlife pests in California. The basic description, behavior, and kind of damage they are likely to cause are given in table 2. Even someone with no training or experience can often identify a pest by thoroughly examining the damaged area. Because feeding signs of many wildlife species are similar, indications such as droppings, tracks, burrows, nests, or food caches are usually important for making a positive species identification.

Four steps lead to a successful wildlife pest control program:

- Correctly identify the species caus-ing or likely to cause the problem.
- Make the area less attractive to the pest by altering the habitat when possible or by improving sanitation.
- Use a control method appropriate to the location, time of year, and other environmental conditions.
- Monitor the site for evidence of rein-festation to determine if additional control is necessary.

The most successful wildlife control programs tailor the techniques used to the situation, whether habitat or behavior manipulation, population reduction, or a combination of these methods are used.

DETECTING THE PRESENCE OF A PEST

Detecting potential wildlife pests and taking steps to prevent damage is easier, safer, less expensive, and less time-consuming than waiting until damage has already occurred. Regular inspection of buildings, gardens, and surrounding areas is the first step in preventing wildlife problems. Your best tool to prevent wildlife damage around your home, garden, and property is to know the potential pests, keep your eyes open for them, and take appropriate actions to prevent damage.

HABITAT MODIFICATION

The availability of food, water, and shelter (cover or living space) are key components that contribute to a pest problem or an increasing pest population of mammals such as rats, voles, tree squirrels, and raccoons, and birds such as cliff swallows and house sparrows. Habitat modification, which often includes improved sanitation and other practical approaches, is effective because it limits access to one or more of the requirements of life—food, water, or shelter. Habitat modification makes the immediate surroundings less attractive to the pest or less conducive to a population increase.

Examples of this approach include

- "animal-proofing" buildings by seal-ing cracks and holes to prevent pests such as rats, house mice, and tree squirrels from entering
- controlling weeds and cleaning up garden debris, which reduces shelter for voles and ground squirrels
- selective pruning of shade trees to increase air circulation, making it less suitable for a starling or black-bird roosting site

Visitation by raccoons and opossums can be dramatically reduced if cat or dog food is not left outdoors overnight. The key is to understand the pest's living requirements and, when possible, selectively reduce or eliminate them. Even the best efforts toward habitat modification and improved sanitation, however, will not completely solve all pest problems.

BEHAVIOR ALTERATION

In many situations, it is possible to alter the behavior of the pest animal in order to eliminate it or frighten it away from an area or reduce its damage or destructiveness. These tactics, which usually affect the senses of the animal, are more useful for some species than others and vary in their degree and duration of effectiveness. Behavioral

TABLE 2.

Common vertebrate pests of California

	DESCRIPTION	BEHAVIOR	DAMAGE
BIRDS			
barn swallow	*Hirundo rustica*. Migratory. 5 to 6 inches (12.5 to 15 cm) long; deeply forked tail. Cup-shaped mud nest is frequently attached to building or other structure.	Uses mud from nearby irrigated fields or natural bodies of water for nest building in late winter or early spring. Nests in pairs; not colonial nesters.	Mud spillage and bird droppings stain and contaminate walls and surfaces beneath nest. Contamination is a nuisance and may spread disease. Damage is minor compared to that of cliff swallows.
blackbird	Many species, family Icteridae. 6 to 16 inches (12.5 to 40.5 cm) long, females smaller. Sharp, pointed bill; plumage iridescent black; female plumage brownish, often with streaked breast. Some species have brightly colored areas of yellow, red, or orange on head or wings.	Gregarious. Flocks range from a few birds to thousands; some species congregate in huge winter roosts.	Eats vegetables (lettuce, peppers, tomatoes, sweet corn) and nuts (sunflowers, almonds).
cliff swallow	*Petrochelidon pyrrhonota*. Migratory. 5 to 6 inches (12.5 to 15 cm) long; tail squared off at the end. Mud nest, frequently attached to buildings, is fully enclosed except for entrance.	Uses mud from nearby irrigated fields or natural bodies of water for nest building in late winter or early spring. Colonial nesters. Feeds on insects in flight.	Extensive mud spillage and bird droppings stain and contaminate wall and surface beneath nest.
crow	*Corvus brachyrhynchos*. A large bird, 17 to 20 inches (43 to 51 cm) long. Coal-black plumage with a rounded tail. Large nests made of sticks are constructed high in trees. Usually found in flocks except when nesting.	Omnivorous. Flocks range from a few birds to a hundred or more when feeding in fields. Congregate in huge winter roosts, often in urban settings.	Droppings seriously contaminate everything below urban roosts. Crop damage includes fruits such as cherries and all kinds of nuts. Corn, milo, and other cereals are often heavily damaged.
crowned sparrow	Two species, from 5¾ to 7 inches (14.5 to 18 cm) long. Typical sparrow coloration, brownish on back, dull grayish breast. Adult white-crowned sparrow (*Zonotrichia leucophrys*): three white and four black alternating strips on crown. Adult golden-crowned sparrow: (*Z. atricapilla*) dull gold crown margined with black.	Forages on ground in grassy and open areas near brush, fencerows, and other such cover.	Feeds on vegetable and fruit crops, especially lettuce, grapes, melons, almonds, and strawberries. Disbuds fruit and nut trees; damages young seedlings in fall and winter.
horned lark	*Eremophila alpestris*. 6½ to 7 inches (16.5 to 18 cm) long. Light brown body above, black band across breast, black strip from bill to eyes; two black "horns" above eyes. Walks with slight sideways swaying of body and fore-and-aft movement of head; does not hop on ground.	Ground-nesting bird found in loose flocks in wide, sparsely vegetated open areas. Normally flies low, swooping up and down slightly.	Feeds on vegetables (lettuce, broccoli, and carrots), melons, and flowers, particularly at seeding stage.
house finch	*Carpodacus mexicanus*. 5 to 5¾ inches (12.5 to 14.5 cm) long. Male has rosy-red head, rump, and breast, brownish back and wings, sides streaked with brown; female lacks red, has brownish body with heavily streaked breast and abdomen.	Well adapted to human environments; often nests in vines on buildings. Sings and chirps from trees, antennas, or posts. Found in variety of habitats, from deserts and open woods to farmlands, suburbs, and farms.	Eats fruits and berries in orchard and garden; attacks seed crops. Disbuds and deflowers fruit and nut trees.
house sparrow	*Passer domesticus*. 5¾ to 6¼ inches (14.5 to 16 cm) long. Male has black bib and bill, white cheeks, and gray cap; female is dull brown above and dingy whitish below without black bib, bill, or gray cap.	Abundant in farmland, cities, and suburbs; lives in loose flocks. Often nests in eaves, vents, or other openings and cavities in buildings.	Eats emerging seedlings, fruits, and buds; damages flowers, newly seeded lawns, and ripening fruit. Droppings deface and contaminate buildings.
magpie, yellow billed	*Pica nuttali*. 16 to 20 inches (40.5 to 51 cm) long; black and white body with long, streaming tail.	Lives in farming areas of California valleys and nearby foothills. Gregarious, nests in colonies. Builds large nest of sticks high in trees near open grasslands or fields.	Feeds on fruits, nuts, grain, and garbage.

	DESCRIPTION	BEHAVIOR	DAMAGE
pigeon	*Columbida livia.* 14 to 15 inches (35.5 to 38 cm) long. Plump-bodied, short-billed; usually blue-gray with whitish rump and red feet. White, brown, or other-colored plumage not uncommon.	Widespread in cities and suburbs. Feeds on seeds, grain, fruits, and insects. Coos intermittently while perched. Roosts in large flocks.	Nests on buildings; may clog drainpipes. Deposits droppings on buildings and cars; contaminates foodstuffs. Transmits disease to humans and domestic animals.
scrub jay	*Aphelocoma californica.* 10 to 12 inches (25.5 to 30.5 cm) long. Head, wings, and tail blue; under parts and back gray; white throat; no crest.	Found throughout California except in deserts and high mountains. Very vocal and noisy. Makes shorts flights ending in sweeping glide.	Eats fruits and nuts.
starling	*Sturnus vulgaris.* 7½ to 8½ inches (19 to 21.5 cm) long. Short tail; long, slender, yellow bill in spring and summer, dark bill in winter; plumage black to purplish-black; heavily speckled in winter.	Abundant in city parks, suburbs, and on farms. Gregarious; uses large communal roosts from late summer until spring. Flies swiftly and directly. Primarily a ground feeder.	Pulls small plants; damages fruit (grapes, cherries, strawberries, and others). Nests in building eaves and other openings; droppings deface buildings.
woodpecker	17 species in California, including sapsuckers (*Sphyrapucys* spp.) and flickers (*Colaptes auratus*). 5¾ to 15 inches (14.5 to 38 cm) long. All have strong, sharply pointed bill for chipping and digging in tree trunks and branches for insects; use stiff tail as a prop. The flicker is a jay-sized woodpecker with brown back and white rump; usually salmon-red under wings, but occasionally yellow.	Most species peck or drum repeatedly on resonant limbs, poles, or drainpipes. Usually undulates in flight, folding wings against the body after each series of flaps. All species nest in excavated holes. Flickers are often seen on the ground eating ants.	Inflicts structural damage, drilling into siding and shingles and under eaves of buildings for food or to excavate nest chamber. Also damages fences, poles, and other wood structures. Drumming on buildings may create annoying noise.
MAMMALS			
bat	Bats can be easily identified by their small bodies connected to a fleshy wing structure. Wingspans can range from 9 to 16 inches (23 to 40.5 cm) and colors vary. They can be solitary or live in large groups and occupy structures, caves, or trees.	Bats are nocturnal and almost exclusively insectivores in North America. They mate in the fall or winter but do not give birth until spring. Bats may migrate or hibernate for as much as 9 months; they can also be found in California throughout the year.	The indoor roosting sites of bats can have several economic and aesthetic effects, often involving public health. Bats have been known to be carriers of ectoparasites, rabies, and histoplasmosis.
deer	Large, split-hoofed ruminants, family Cervidae. 3 to 3½ feet (0.9 to 1.1 m) tall at shoulder. Reddish in summer, blue-gray in winter; males have antlers that are shed each year.	Active in the mornings and evenings. Moves singly or in small groups; follows definite trails.	Feeds on shrub and tree twigs, buds, grasses, and vegetables. Males polish their antlers by beating and scraping tree and shrub limbs. Invades gardens and orchards, eating and trampling fruits and vegetables.
deer mice	Deer mice can be identified by their white feet and undersides. Their bicolored tails can be as long as their head and body and they have larger eyes and ears than house mice.	The most abundant mammal in North America, deer mice occupy most of the continent. They are nocturnal and build their nests underground, aboveground, or in trees, breeding in the spring and fall. Deer mice are primarily seed eaters, but they also consume fruits, insects, fungi, and green plants.	Deer mice enter homes, build nests, and damage furniture, clothing, or other material they use for nests. They dig up seeds from gardens or flowerbeds, and have been found to carry hantavirus.
ground squirrel	Two species in California: California ground squirrel (*Spermophilus beecheyi*) and Belding or Oregon ground squirrel (*S. beldingi*). The California ground squirrel is larger, with a head and body from 9 to 11 inches (23 to 28 cm) long and a somewhat bushy tail. The Belding ground squirrel's head and body measures 8 to 9 inches (20.5 to 23 cm), with a relatively short and flat-looking tail, about 2½ to 3 inches (6.5 to 7.5 cm) long. Both have brownish-gray head and body; may have conspicuous dark triangle on back between shoulders.	Lives in colonies in underground burrows. Diurnal; hibernates in summer and winter. Feeds mostly on the ground, but can climb trees. Diet depends on the season: prefers green vegetation in spring, nuts and seeds in the summer.	Eats fruits and nuts such as almonds, apples, apricots, walnuts, oranges, as well as a variety of vegetables. Burrows weaken ground above. Chews on plastic irrigation pipe, trees, and shrubs. Can transmit disease to humans and other animals.

	DESCRIPTION	BEHAVIOR	DAMAGE
meadow vole	*Microtus californicus.* 4 to 5 inches (10 to 12.5 cm) long. Stocky body; short tail and limbs; small eyes; ears concealed in thick fur.	Lives in burrow and runway system in heavy grass or weed cover (common in hay meadows, irrigated pastures, ditch banks, roadsides, and alfalfa fields). Seldom found in sparse cover. Eats seeds, leaves, and succulent, fleshy vegetation. Active day and night, year round. Not found in buildings.	Eats grasses, vegetable seedlings, root crops, and a variety of vegetables. Girdles trees, shrubs, and ornamentals. Runways and burrows destroy landscaping.
mole	4 *Scapanus* species in California. Most common is broad-footed mole (*S. latimanus);* head and body 5 to 6 inches (12.5 to 15 cm) long. Pointed snout and 1½-inch (4-cm) tail; eyes and ears not visible; soft thick fur, blackish-brown to black; tail slightly haired.	Rarely comes above ground; lives and feeds in underground tunnels. Feeds on insects and earthworms. One species, the Townsend's mole (*S. townsendii),* may eat roots and tubers. Active day and night. Pushes up low ridges and volcanolike mounds as it burrows just under surface.	Burrows and ridges disfigure gardens, lawns, and landscaped areas. Can damage roots and tubers.
opossum	*Didelphis virginiana.* About the size of large adult house cat, 2 to 3 feet (0.6 to 0.6 m) long, including the tail; weighs up to 15 pounds (6.8 kg). Relatively long fur that appears unkempt, not smooth. Face is pointed with elongated muzzle; mouth full of sharp teeth; prehensile tail is hairless and scaly.	Only marsupial in North America. Active year around, mostly nocturnal; thrives very well in urban and suburban environments. Lives beneath structures such as buildings, decks, porches, and sheds. Omnivorous.	Feeds on vegetables and a wide variety of fruits and nuts. Raids pet food dishes, compost piles, and garbage cans. Can severely injure pets.
pocket gopher	*Thomomys* spp. Stocky rodents 6 to 12 inches (15 to 30.5 cm) long. Soft, fine fur, various shades of brown; small eyes, ears, and flattened head; external cheek pouches; long, curved front claws.	Lives and feeds in underground burrow system, usually one gopher per burrow system. Seldom seen above ground. Pushes dirt from excavations to surface, producing mounds. Active year round.	Mounds cover plants, ruin lawns and landscaping. Feeds on roots of trees, shrubs, and garden plants. Gnaws on plastic irrigation pipe and underground cables.
rabbit	Three rabbits are common in California: the black-tailed jackrabbit (*Lepus californicus),* the cottontail (*Sylvilagus audubonii),* and the brush rabbit (*S. bachmani).* The jackrabbit is 17 to 22 inches (43 to 56 cm) long, with ears 5 to 7 inches (12.5 to 18 cm) long and tail 2 to 3 inches (5 to 7.5 cm) long. Cottontails and brush rabbits have smaller bodies and shorter ears, with short, cottony tails.	Jackrabbits are primarily nocturnal; very fast runners, preferring open spaces; seldom inhabit dense brush or woods. Cottontails and brush rabbits are usually found in or near brush or other cover.	Feeds on a variety of garden crops as well as bark, buds, and twigs. Girdles small trees, shrubs, and vines.
raccoon	*Procyon lotor.* Heavily furred, stocky mammal about 2 to 3 feet (0.6 to 0.9 m) long, weighing 10 to 30 pounds (4.5 to 13.5 kg). Distinctive markings of black mask over eyes and alternating light and dark rings around the tail.	Nocturnal; active year round but may hole up in dens during periods of severe winter weather. Adapts well to urban and suburban environments. Often dens beneath homes, decks, or accessible outbuildings, attics, and chimneys. Omnivorous.	Eats fruits, berries, nuts, corn, and grain, as well as the eggs and young of ground-nesting birds. Scavenges from garbage cans and compost piles. Can damage houses, decks, sheds, and other structures.
skunk	About the size of a house cat, 2 to 3 feet (0.6 to 0.9 m) long, weighing 10 to 30 pounds (4.5 to 13.5 kg). Long, dense black fur with white stripes, spots, or other patterns; long bushy tail. Well known for characteristic defensive odor. The striped skunk (*Mephitis mephitis*) is the most widely distributed in California; spotted skunks (*Spilogale gracilis*) are also found.	Primarily nocturnal. Usually solitary except for mothers with offspring; can be active year around. Found in suburban residential areas as well as more natural rural habitats. Rather timid; not generally aggressive but will take a stand, spraying foul-smelling musk if threatened.	Sprays nauseating scent and can carry rabies. Digs holes in lawns and gardens for insects. Feeds on a variety of fruits and nuts, corn, and other garden crops.

	DESCRIPTION	BEHAVIOR	DAMAGE
tree squirrel	Four common species in California: eastern fox squirrel (Sciurus niger), eastern gray squirrel (S. carolinensis), western gray squirrel (S. griseus), and Douglas squirrel (Tamiasciurus douglasii). Depending on species, head and body from 7 to 15 inches (18 to 38 cm) long; bushy tail 5 to 14 inches (12.5 to 35.5 cm) long; similar to ground squirrel.	Diurnal, year round; rarely venture far from trees. Nests in holes in trees or builds twig and leaf nests in crotches or branches of trees.	Feeds on nuts (green and ripe walnuts and almonds), fruits (oranges, apples, and avocados), seeds, and tree cambium beneath bark. Gnaws telephone lines and wooden buildings. Invades attics.
Rats and Mice			
Norway rat	Rattus norvegicus. Head and body heavy and thick, 12 to 18 inches (30.5 to 45.5 cm) long including tail. Tail shorter than head and body; small eyes and ears; blunt snout.	Found almost everywhere humans live. Colonial, in burrows; uses networks of runways. Often burrows along foundations of buildings or beneath rubbish piles. Omnivorous and nocturnal.	Eats a variety of fruits, vegetables, and nuts; feeds on anything edible. Urine and feces contaminate foodstuffs, carries disease. Gnaws on wood and other materials; can damage structures.
roof rat	Rattus rattus. Head and body light and slender, 7 to 8 inches (18 to 20.5 cm) long; naked tail 8 to 10 inches (20.5 to 25.5 cm) long. Naked tail is longer than head and body. Large eyes and ears; black or dark brown body.	Found chiefly in and around buildings. Builds nests in dense vegetation (ivy, shrubs, etc.). In buildings, usually found in upper parts (attic or ceiling space between floors). Omnivorous, but prefers fresh fruits, nuts, and vegetables.	Eats almost any fruit, nut, or vegetable; strips bark and gnaws trees and shrubs. Can damage structures. Carries disease and contaminates stored foods.
house mouse	Mus musculus. 5 to 7 inches (12.5 to 18 cm) long. Tail slightly longer than head and body. Light brown to dark gray; almost hairless, scaly tail.	Breeds year round. Usually found in and around buildings, but also in open fields in burrows. Omnivorous.	Feeds on anything edible, especially grain, seeds, and nuts. Can damage structures. Destroys and contaminates stored foods. Carries disease.
REPTILES			
rattlesnake	Crotalus spp. Up to 6 feet (1.8 m) long and 3½ inches (7.5 cm) in diameter. Key characteristic is triangular head; rattle on end of tail with series of interlocking horny segments. Rattle can be broken off; lack of rattle is not an indication that a snake is not a rattlesnake.	Hunts for prey in or near brushy or grassy areas. When inactive, seeks rock outcroppings, rodent burrows, or hides beneath low objects. Hibernates in winter months in some areas; active in the spring when it suns itself in early morning along trails or other open places.	Venomous bite is seldom fatal but extremely painful, leading to severe medical trauma. Children and pets are especially vulnerable.

alteration is often the best approach to bird control because it is not harmful and few other methods are available for these species, many of which are protected by law.

Behavior-modifying devices such as electrically charged wire, bird-repelling spikes, and sweeping arms for keeping birds from alighting on building ledges or billboards remain effective indefinitely if properly maintained. Tacky or sticky materials may be effective for months but must be replenished. Visual repellents such as hawk kites, flagging, and twirling and reflecting devices may have some short-term effects on birds, but birds quickly habituate to them. Depending on the species, sound-producing devices such as distress calls may frighten birds more than explosive devices such as propane cannons. Chemical repellents based on taste or odors are available to deter pests from damaging plants; some are more effective than others. Unfortunately, most animal species soon learn that repellents are not actually harmful, or the effects of the repellent soon dissipate, allowing the animals to continue to feed. Animals can also habituate to devices such as revolving lights. Most behavior alteration methods or devices are effective for a relatively short period. If different methods are rotated or used in a sequence, the desired effects can be prolonged.

POPULATION REDUCTION

Toxic baits, traps, or shooting may be necessary to reduce pest numbers to more acceptable levels. Since the animals that survive continue to reproduce as long as they have abundant food, water, and shelter, these lethal methods should be accompanied whenever possible by sanitation, pest-proof construction and exclusion, and other appropriate techniques of habitat or behavior modification. When food and shelter are continuously available, as is the case in many gardens, periodic population control measures may need to be scheduled for certain pests.

NATURAL CONTROL

In addition to the presence or absence of food, water, and shelter, predators, diseases, and parasites also play a role in regulating population densities, as do biotic factors such as stress, competition, and fertility. Inclement weather may help suppress certain pests. One or more of these factors prevent indefinite increases in numbers in all populations. Because animal populations are self-limiting, one management alternative when confronted with a pest is to take no action. Experience has shown, however, that by the time the population limits itself, it may already have severely damaged your home and garden.

BIOLOGICAL CONTROL

Encouraging, using, or allowing natural enemies (predators, parasites, or diseases) to control a pest is commonly referred to as biological control. While this approach has worked for a number of insect pests, there are very few successful examples for wildlife pests. None are available for controlling wildlife in gardens or around structures. Although a variety of predators such as hawks, owls, foxes, and coyotes feed on wildlife pests, few such predators are commonly found in populated areas. Even when present, they are usually unable to keep pest populations below damaging levels. Some gardeners encourage predators such as barn owls and build nest boxes to encourage them to inhabit the area. While this can be of benefit to barn owls and can add wildlife interest to your garden, it is rarely, if ever, effective in preventing rodent damage.

WILDLIFE PEST CONTROL EQUIPMENT AND SUPPLIES

Local retail outlets, such as farm supply stores, hardware stores, nurseries, and garden shops, often stock wildlife pest control supplies. Internet searches offer another source of information on the availability of equipment and supplies. Some county agricultural commissioners and public health departments sell or distribute wildlife pest control materials, usually baits for rodent control. If you cannot locate appropriate control materials, contact your University of California Cooperative Extension office, usually listed under "County Offices" in the telephone directory, for further information.

DISPOSAL OF CARCASSES

Carcasses of killed vertebrate pests may harbor parasites and diseases and must be disposed of with care. An easy and safe method for smaller animals is to use a large disposable plastic bag (fig. 1). Insert your hand into the bag and grasp the carcass. Invert the bag over the carcass. With the carcass now inside, seal the bag tightly with string or a twist-tie. Dispose of the carcass in a garbage can with a tight-fitting lid.

FIGURE 1.

Dispose of carcasses in a heavy-duty disposable plastic bag.

Birds

FIGURE 2.

White-crowned sparrow.

*C*ALIFORNIA IS HOME to numerous species of birds representing several dozen families. Individual birds of some of these families have little fear of humans or our activities and readily visit our gardens and even attempt to share our dwellings. This section covers particular bird species that are most apt to damage gardens and home orchards or to damage or deface homes in a substantial way. While several other species, including Canada geese, gulls, and vultures, may conflict with human interests, the problems they create are limited geographically and often require community rather than individual effort to resolve.

FIGURE 3.

House finch, also commonly called a linnet.

FIGURE 4.

European starling.

FIGURE 5.

Brewer's blackbird.

Sparrows, Finches, Jays, Crows, and Other Common Birds

Many species of birds are frequent visitors to gardens. Much of the time they pose no threat as they forage for insects and seeds, but a few birds, during certain periods in the garden's growth cycle, can cause significant problems. Birds such as white-crowned sparrows (*Zonotrichia* spp.) (fig. 2) can unearth and eat seeds or feed on newly sprouted seedlings. Occasionally species such as the house finch (*Carpodacus mexicanus*) (fig. 3), also called a linnet, eat buds and flowers, reducing fruit set. Probably the greatest damage occurs when birds such as house finches, European starlings (*Sturnus vulgaris*) (fig. 4), and blackbirds (*Euphagus* spp.) (fig. 5) feed on ripening berries and fruits (figs. 6–14). Nut crops are also susceptible and are favored by scrub jays (*Aphelocoma californica*) (fig. 15), crows (*Corvus brachyrhynchos*), and magpies (*Pica* spp). (fig. 16).

FIGURE 6.

House finch damage to peach.

FIGURE 7.

House finch damage to apples.

FIGURE 8.

House finch damage to cherries.

FIGURE 9.

House finch damage to strawberry.

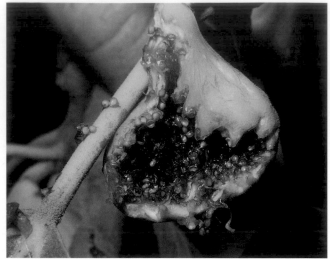

FIGURE 10.

House finch damage to fig.

FIGURE 12.

Starling damage to strawberry.

FIGURE 13.

Starling damage to apples.

FIGURE 14.

Blackbird damage to garbanzo beans.

FIGURE 11.

Starling damage to grapes. Note that starlings remove the entire grape from the bunch.

While a select group of birds damages gardens, other birds favor the use of buildings for loafing, roosting, and nesting. California's most common bird pests of the garden and home are given in table 2, which includes a brief description of each bird, its general behavioral characteristics, and the kind or type of damage or problem the bird causes. Control methods described in this chapter, for the most part, are useful regardless of the species of bird involved. Cliff swallows (*Petrochelidon pyrrhonota*) and woodpeckers (family Picidae), because of their unique nesting habits, are discussed in separate chapters.

FIGURE 15.

Scrub jay.

FIGURE 16.

Yellow-billed magpie.

LEGAL RESTRAINTS OF CONTROL

The U.S. Code of Federal Regulations classifies most of the birds that cause problems in gardens as migratory nongame birds. As such, they are protected from indiscriminate control. Only European starlings, house sparrows (*Passer domesticus*), and pigeons (*Columbida livia*) may be controlled without a permit. However, no permit is needed to frighten or exclude depredating or nuisance birds from the house or garden unless they are nesting.

CONTROL METHODS

Of the several approaches to solving bird problems in gardens, exclusion, frightening, and repellents are the most commonly used. Anticipating the problem is critical because damage is often sudden and catastrophic. Birds may descend without warning and wipe out all your cherries in one day or devour newly planted sweet peas before you are aware of the birds' arrival. Preventive action is the key to success. Control methods are somewhat more numerous for resolving damage or nuisance caused by pigeons, house sparrows, and starlings loafing or nesting on buildings (fig. 17). These methods include sticky repellents, bird projections, electrical shocking devices, and in some cases, traps.

Many gardeners enjoy having birds frequent their gardens, and some even plant trees, shrubs, and perennials that attract them. Others enjoy providing food, nest boxes, and sources of water in fountains or bird baths. Encouraging the presence of birds does not mean that you have to give up the crop of cherries, peaches, or almonds or avoid planting certain annuals susceptible to bird damage. Exclusion by netting or screening provides an excellent bird-friendly environment in which birds and garden plantings can coexist, and it is one of the best and most consistently effective methods for controlling bird pests in homes and gardens. When selecting fruit trees to plant, keep in mind that dwarf fruit trees are much easier to net (fig. 18).

Habitat Modification

Gardens are attractive to birds, and not much can be done to modify the habitat to discourage them. In some situations, thinning the branches of large shade trees may discourage nighttime roosting by starlings, blackbirds, and crows. Thinning sometimes also makes the tree less suitable for nesting.

Adequately pruning shrubs to prevent overgrowth tends to reduce cover for some birds, as does eliminating brush piles that can attract them. By observing the activity of the birds in your garden, you may be able to identify and remove or modify the things that attract them.

Exclusion

Exclusion is a consistently effective method of reducing or eliminating bird damage in the garden. Purchase lightweight ¾-inch-mesh plastic netting for this purpose. Suspend the netting over berry vines or small trees to protect the fruit from bird damage (figs. 19–20).

Build a frame out of plastic pipe or wood to support the netting above the seedbeds to keep the netting from reducing or interfering with plant

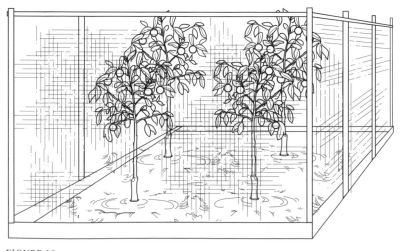

FIGURE 17.

Pigeons loafing or nesting on window ledges create a mess and may expose occupants to diseases and ectoparasites.

FIGURE 18.

Dwarf fruit trees can easily be netted using a rigid frame.

FIGURE 19.

Netting can be suspended from a tall frame, as over this cherry tree.

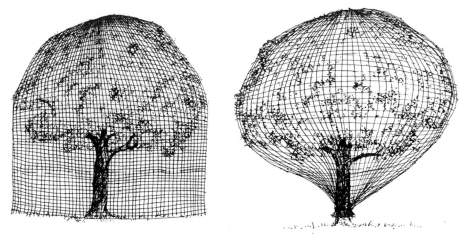

FIGURE 20.

Two examples of bird netting over trees. The netting must deny access to birds at ground level.

growth (fig. 21). The netting can be loosened and folded back to permit harvest. This method can also protect crops from rabbits, squirrels, and neighborhood cats. Arches made of concrete reinforcement bar or long pliable wood also work well to support netting. These should be able to be lifted off, or the netting pulled back, to allow for attending to the plants. To keep birds from getting beneath the netting, make sure that the netting reaches the ground or is tied tightly to the trunk. Do not be careless in placing the net; keep it taut and tight fitting, since birds can become entangled in loose netting. Metal wire mesh or aviary wire row caps can also be effective for protecting rows of seedlings, and they are stiff enough to not require a support frame (fig. 22). The mesh should be secured to a wooden frame. Row caps be lifted off as the plants mature and can be used year after year. Inverted plastic strawberry baskets can also serve this purpose (fig. 23).

Netting can also solve problems associated with birds that loaf, roost, or nest on buildings. An entire roof can be netted to prevent bird loafing; stretch the netting taut a foot or so above the roof. Netting (¾-inch) can also be installed under eaves (see fig. 30), rafters, and over inner courtyards. Other methods to exclude birds from buildings include bird projections, spikelike devices that are permanently secured along ledges to prevent birds from landing or nesting. Electric shocking devices, although more expensive, are also effective. They are used mostly on large commercial buildings and are generally installed by bird control specialists. Be sure the device is made for repelling birds. Homemade shocking devices can present serious hazards if not constructed properly.

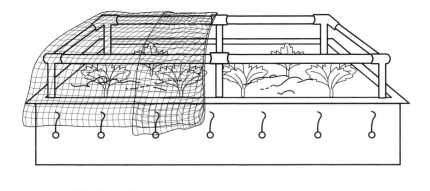

FIGURE 21.

Bird netting (¾-inch mesh) draped and secured over a framework of PVC pipe to protect a crop.

Frightening

Twisted reflective tape stretched 6 to 8 inches (15 to 20.5 cm) above the length of a row of seedlings or strawberry plants can effectively frighten birds away when the wind causes the reflective tape to shimmer and shine (fig. 24). Streamers of reflective tape 2 to 3 feet (0.6 to 0.9 m) long attached directly to trees can reduce bird damage to fruit, especially where protection is needed only for a few days to a week prior to harvest. A row of tin can lids strung on a wire also frightens birds (fig. 25), as do devices such as large eyespot balloons. The effectiveness of these frightening devices usually decreases as birds become accustomed to them. For best results, frequently change the method used.

Many models of predators and reflective gadgets are marketed to frighten birds, but their effectiveness is, at best, of short duration. Loud sound-producing devices are rarely practical because the noise they create also disturbs people. Inaudible high-frequency sound devices are ineffective on birds. The sound of a portable radio placed near a crop frightens birds away for a day or two but rarely longer. This can buy you time to install netting.

Repellents

Certain chemical repellents are marketed to control birds in situations such as repelling geese from turf. Most bird repellents, however, are not registered for use on edible commodities such as fruit or vegetables. Repellents based on objectionable tastes, odors, or learned aversions rarely provide gardeners with appreciable protection against birds.

Nontoxic sticky or tacky repellents can play a significant role in discouraging birds from roosting or loafing on buildings. Birds do not like the feel of these sticky or tacky materials, which do not trap the birds but rather make them uncomfortable and encourage them to avoid the treated surfaces. A wide variety of these materials is available. They are generally applied with a caulking gun in a manner prescribed by the label, although some can be applied as a spray. Although they can be effective, these repellents may stain painted surfaces and may spread in hot weather. Treated surfaces also

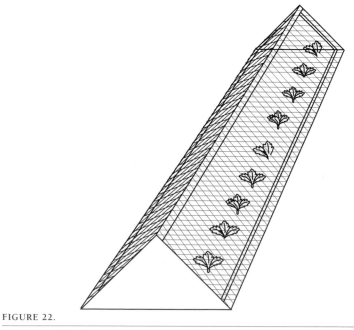

FIGURE 22.

Row caps made of wire mesh can also protect sensitive seedlings from bird depredation and animal interference.

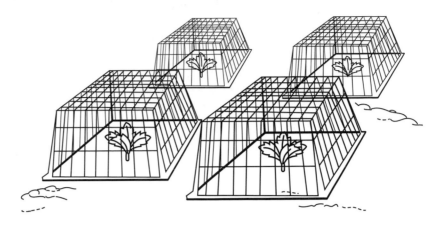

FIGURE 23.

Inverted strawberry baskets can help protect young seedlings from birds.

FIGURE 24.

Shiny plastic reflective tape stretched over garden rows can effectively frighten birds. Multiple streamers attached to posts can also be effective for short periods of time.

collect dust that, over time, reduces the effectiveness of control.

Trapping

Trapping is rarely a solution to bird problems in a garden because birds are highly mobile and new arrivals quickly move in if the bird population is reduced. About the only exception is when house sparrows or pigeons persist in nesting or loafing on a building. In this situation, trapping may offer a possible solution. Live-catch traps for pigeons and house sparrows are commercially available. Live trapping, however, presents the problem of disposing of the trapped birds. Because of their homing ability, releasing them elsewhere is not a viable solution. Only starlings, pigeons, and house sparrows can be trapped and destroyed without a permit.

Other Control Methods

Birds can sometimes be discouraged from flying into windows by taping hawk silhouettes on the glass or suspending a spread-winged hawk model in front of the window. As a last resort, unobtrusive bird netting can be stretched taut a few inches in front of the window, softening the

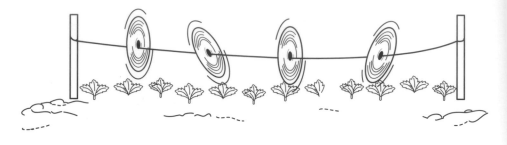

FIGURE 25.

Tin can lids or recycled CDs strung on a wire over a row of seedlings to frighten birds.

impact of a strike and safeguarding the birds. Allowing pet cats and dogs to run freely in a yard discourages some birds, but this is not always a solution. Shooting nonprotected birds such as pigeons may be effective in rural areas where it is safe and not prohibited.

MONITORING GUIDELINES

The best way to monitoring potential pest birds is to watch your garden and residence closely. Learn to identify the birds you see and know what damage or problems they may cause. Be prepared to initiate a plan of action to minimize a developing problem.

CLIFF SWALLOWS

Seven members of the swallow family (Hirundinidae) breed in California, but only the cliff swallow (*Petrochelidon pyrrhonota*) (fig. 26) and, much less frequently, the barn swallow (*Hirundo rustica*), become significant problems by constructing their mud nests on dwellings or other structures.

The cliff swallow is a small bird, about 5 to 6 inches (12.5 to 15 cm) long with a squared-off tail, that nests in colonies (fig. 27). The barn swallow can be differentiated from the cliff swallow by the barn swallow's deeply forked tail, and unlike cliff swallows it does not nest in colonies. Cliff swallows migrate to South America each winter and return in the spring, generally to their previous nesting site or place of birth. From time to time new nesting colonies are started and old colonies may be abandoned. Once a colony is started, it is likely to grow each year if nothing is done to discourage nesting. Since swallows make mud nests, they select buildings, bridges, overpasses, or other structures near a good source of mud, such as irrigated agricultural crops or natural bodies of open water. The nests are fully enclosed, except for the entrance near the top (barn swallow nests are cup-shaped with an open top) (figs. 28–29). Swallows feed on insects while in flight, so a high population of flying insects is required to sustain them. Cliff swallows can cause problems when their nests are constructed on buildings. The appearance of nests may be unsightly, and residual mud and bird droppings deface the building beneath the nest colony. If the nest is above a stairway, sidewalk, or door entrance, this contamination is not only unsightly and a health hazard but is also a slippery hazard when wet. Daily cleaning often becomes necessary. After the nesting season, the mud nest may fall off or be dislodged by wind, high humidity, or rain.

FIGURE 26.

Cliff swallow.

FIGURE 27.

Colony of cliff swallows.

FIGURE 28.

Paired-off cliff swallows in partially constructed nests.

FIGURE 29.

A finished cliff swallow nest is fully enclosed except at the entrance.

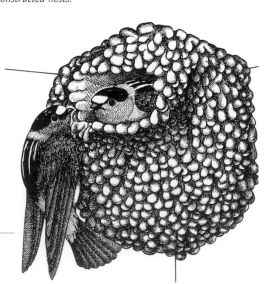

LEGAL RESTRAINTS OF CONTROL

All swallows are included under the Migratory Bird Treaty Act of 1918 as migratory insectivorous birds and as such are protected by state and federal regulations. The California Department of Fish and Game (DFG), the enforcement agency of these regulations, considers February 15 to September 1 to be the swallow nesting season. During this nesting season, completed nests cannot be tampered with, knocked down, or washed away without a permit. Outside of these dates, a permit is not required to remove the nests. During nesting, a permit authorizing nest removal will be issued only if it can be justified by strong compelling reasons; the U.S. Fish and Wildlife Service (FWS) issues such permits. For example, justification might include a health or safety hazard posed by a nesting colony situated near a doorway or entrance, a loading area of a warehouse, a food processing facility, or at an airport if aircraft or maintenance safety are impaired.

If eggs or young are in the nest when a permit is requested, the application will probably be denied. It is best to request the permit during the nonbreeding season and well before spring nest construction begins. Past history of problems at the site is taken into consideration. Permits are issued for one season. The permit authorizes the permittee or their employee(s) to use specified methods to remove the nests. The number of nests removed must be reported within 10 days after the permit expires.

CONTROL METHODS

Because swallows enjoy protected status, few options are available for controlling them. Exclusion is by far the most acceptable method; modifying building surfaces before nests are attached offers an alternative

FIGURE 30.

Bird netting to exclude cliff swallows.

nest removal generally requires many days because the birds persistently attempt to rebuild nests for much of the nesting season. More often than not they will return the following year, and the removal process must be repeated unless other measures are taken to prevent or inhibit future nest building. If a permit is obtained it generally specifies the allowed methods of removal.

Exclusion

Any method that denies physical access to a nest site can be referred to as exclusion. A permit is not required for this method if the exclusion is conducted during the nonnesting season or before the birds arrive in the spring. Plastic or fabric-type netting with mesh no larger than ¾ inch (19 mm) can provide a barrier restricting access to the nest site or potential nest site (fig. 30). The netting should be stretched taut from the eaves back to the wall about 2 to 3 feet (0.6 to 0.9 m) below the eaves, without obstructing windows or doors if present (fig. 31). Individuals experiencing a swallow problem often resist stretching netting over portions of their homes because they perceive it as a visual blight. If properly installed, netting is barely noticeable from a few yards away. Leave the netting in place for a couple of years or until you no longer see swallows scouting for a site to build nests at the beginning of the breeding season. Generally, the entire length of a building must be netted, rather than just the area where nesting previously occurred. This is to prevent the swallows from building new nests a few feet beyond the netting.

Hanging a curtain of netting from the eaves a few inches away from the wall has been reported to discourage swallows from using a nesting site (fig. 32). The curtain should extend downward about 2 feet (0.6 m) and be kept taut by monofilament fishing line

in some situations. Daily hosing of the area where the birds land usually discourages them from building a nest. Most other methods are either ineffective or not permitted. Nest removal, under permit, is rarely authorized for a nuisance problem.

Nest Removal

During the nonbreeding season or prior to nest completion, nests may be removed by water pressure using a hose or by striking them with a long pole. Swallows have a strong attachment to their selected nest site and are not easily deterred. During nest building,

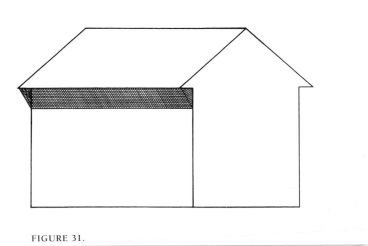

FIGURE 31.

Mount netting from the outer edge of the eaves down to the side of the building. Attach the netting with wooden dowels and hooks (insert).

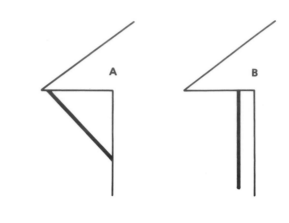

FIGURE 32.

Three methods of excluding cliff swallows. A: Stretch netting from the outer edge of the eaves down to the side of the building. B: Attach a curtain of netting parallel to the side of the building.

attached to the bottom and secured to L-shaped brackets. If the installation of netting is too difficult for the property owner, a professional wildlife pest control operator can be hired for the task. They are experienced in these types of jobs and have the proper equipment for the installation. They may also offer some other options, such as installing smooth fiberglass panels or clear plastic sheeting to form a curvature over the angles where the eaves meet the wall, inhibiting nest construction. Other very smooth materials affixed to the wall, such as glass or stainless steel sheeting, can present a surface on which birds are unable to light and secure their mud nests.

Other Control Methods

Most other methods to prevent swallow nesting are unsuccessful or unproved. Unsuccessful methods include installing hawk, owl, or snake models and using various reflective or spinning devices. Unproved methods include taped alarm calls, noisemakers, revolving lights, and high-frequency sound. Sharp metal or plastic bird projectors that prevent birds from roosting on ledges have been used with somewhat inconsistent results; they offer no benefit over netting. There are no effective chemical repellents, and sticky bird repellents are not recommended. Cliff swallows cannot be harmed in any way; shooting, trapping, or using toxicants of any type is illegal.

MONITORING GUIDELINES

Swallows are so visible that monitoring guidelines are generally not needed; their presence will immediately be noticed. Once a pair of birds nests at a site, more birds are apt to appear the following year. Early intervention is prudent. Completed nests constructed between February 15 and September 1 cannot be disturbed or removed without a permit.

WOODPECKERS

Woodpeckers (fig. 33), including sapsuckers (*Sphyrapucys* spp.) and flickers (*Colaptes auratus*), belong to an interesting and well-known group of birds in the family Picidae. Seventeen species are found in California, two of which are California-listed endangered species. Woodpeckers vary from about 5¾ to 15 inches (14.5 to 38 cm) in length and usually have brightly contrasting coloration. Most males have some red on the head, and black and white markings are common on many species. They have short legs with two sharp-clawed backward-pointed toes and stiff tail feathers that serve as support. These physical traits permit them to cling easily to trees or wood surfaces. (They have stout, sharply pointed beaks and use a long tongue to extract insect larvae and adults from wood crevices.) Because they depend to a great extent on trees for shelter and food, woodpeckers are commonly found in or on the fringes of wooded or forested areas.

Woodpeckers come into conflict with people when they peck wooden dwellings in search of food or use them for territorial or social drumming or nest construction. These activities can create not only disturbing noises but, more significantly, structural damage. Pecking damage can occur on wooden siding, eaves, or trim boards. Cedar and redwood siding seem most vulnerable, especially if it is a rustic veneer-type plywood. Reverse board and batten veneer plywood is especially subject to damage because gaps resulting from the manufacturing process provide hidden spaces that harbor insects that attract woodpeckers in search of food. Characteristic damage consists of a series of small holes in a row. Woodpeckers can also peck all the way through wood siding and build nests in the wall cavity. Exploratory pecking is commonplace, with only a fraction of it having a function or purpose. Damage tends to be localized on houses in or near

FIGURE 33.

Acorn woodpeckers (Melanerpes form-micivorus).

FIGURE 34.

Sapsuckers peck parallel rows of holes into the limbs and trunks of trees.

FIGURE 35.

Acorn woodpecker damage to a fence post.

natural wooded areas and most often occurs in suburban or rural settings.

Part of a woodpecker's breeding behavior is an incessant rhythmic tapping or repetitive drumming with their bills on wood or other hard surfaces as a way of proclaiming their breeding territory and social significance. The birds select drumming surfaces that resonate loudly. They frequently bypass wood and use metal gutters and downspouts, television antennae, or metal ventilators on roofs. Both male and female woodpeckers are involved in drumming. This activity may become very annoying to household residents, especially if it starts in the early-morning hours.

Gardeners and landscapers are sometimes confronted with a series of rows of small holes pecked through the bark of a tree trunk or tree limb by a sapsucker seeking food (fig. 34). Over time, this continuous activity extends the number of rows of holes, and the resulting loss of sap may weaken the tree and provide access for harmful insects or plant diseases, and can lead to the death of the tree. Some species of woodpeckers feed on fruits, berries, and nuts, but this feeding is only rarely considered a significant problem.

Acorn woodpeckers (*Melanerpes formicivorus*) drill numerous holes in buildings, wooden fence posts, utility poles, and old tree snags, in which they place individual acorns (fig. 35). This woodpecker may also take a quicker approach and wedge acorns beneath wooden shakes or shingles, which can be very destructive. Hundreds or thousands of acorns may be cached in this way in a single season.

LEGAL RESTRAINTS OF CONTROL

All woodpeckers are protected under the Migratory Bird Treaty Act of 1918 as migratory insectivorous birds and are classified as nongame birds by the state of California. Two California woodpeckers, the Gila woodpecker (*Melanerpes uropygialis*) and the gilded northern flicker (*Colaptes auratus chrysoides*), are California-listed endangered species and are offered greater protection. When warranted, woodpeckers other than endangered species can be killed but only under a permit issued by the Law Enforcement Division of the U.S. Fish and Wildlife Service on recommendation of USDA-APHIS-Wildlife Services personnel. Generally there must be a good case to justify issuance of a permit, and the permit process is time-consuming. Control methods that do not harm birds or an active nest are allowed except for the two endangered species mentioned above; they cannot be harassed or bothered in any way. Exclusion, if installed before the endangered birds appear in the area, is permissible. For more information on these and other endangered species, see the California DFG Web site at http://www.dfg.ca.gov/.

CONTROL METHODS

Several methods can prevent woodpecker damage or frighten them from a site. Physical exclusion is by far the most effective. More often than not, frightening or repellents fail to provide the desired result.

Exclusion

Using netting to prevent woodpeckers from gaining access to wood siding or other wood surfaces is the method of choice for stopping damage to buildings. Lightweight plastic ¾-inch (19-mm) bird netting can be stretched from the eaves to a lower point on the building (see fig. 36). Alternatively, the netting can be stretched over any flat surface subject to damage, leaving at least 3 inches (7.5 cm) of space between the netting and damaged surface so that the birds cannot cause further damage through the mesh. Netting of the appropriate type and color, when properly installed, is barely visible from a distance of a few yards and offers a long-term solution to prevent subsequent damage. The entire side of a building may have to be netted to prevent the birds from pecking beyond the netted area.

Installing extensive netting may be a bigger task than some homeowners want to assume, especially if it involves a two-story building. In this case, it may be advisable to call a bird control professional. Netting is increasingly used to curtail woodpecker damage because it consistently provides the desired result.

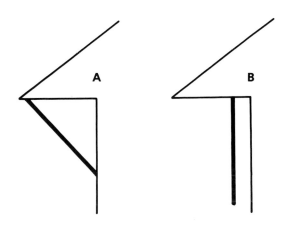

FIGURE 36.

Two methods of using ¾-inch bird netting to prevent woodpecker damage to the side of a building.
A: Stretch netting from the outer edge of the eaves down to the side of the building. B: Attach a curtain
of netting parallel to the side of the building.

Sections of lightweight sheet metal or ¼-inch (6.5-mm) hardware cloth may be fastened directly over woodpecker-damaged areas. If done at the first sign of damage, the bird may be discouraged and move on to another location. Metal sheeting, wire mesh, or poultry wire can be painted to match the siding. This method is most useful where only one or a few relatively small areas have been damaged. Wire mesh can also be wrapped around tree trunks or limbs being damaged by sapsuckers, often solving this problem. In most cases, a large area must be protected with mesh to prevent woodpeckers from moving to a nearby area and begin pecking again.

Frightening Devices

Plastic twirlers or windmills fastened to eaves and aluminum foil or brightly colored plastic strips hung from trees or eaves can repel woodpeckers by movement and reflection but their effectiveness is inconsistent. Models of hawks, owls, and snakes do not frighten woodpeckers. However, a battery-powered sound-activated model of a giant spider has recently received some acclaimed good results for frightening woodpeckers. When the bird pecks on the siding it activates the cup-sized spider to run up a string, and this motion frightens the bird. Attaching several of these spiders to the eaves has reportedly given good results. This is possible only if the woodpecker has not become well attached to a particular location. Once established, woodpeckers can be very persistent and are not easily driven from their territory or selected pecking site.

Repellents

Many chemicals with objectionable tastes or odors have been tested for repelling woodpeckers with little or no success. The search continues, and it is possible that in the future an effective material will be found.

Sticky or tacky bird repellents such as Tanglefoot can be effective if applied to sections of thin plywood and placed over the damaged area. These substances do not entrap the birds; rather, the birds dislike the tacky footing. Applying bird repellents can sometimes be an effective solution to sapsucker attacks on trees.

Other Methods

Woodpeckers may be killed only with a permit, which usually specifies trapping or shooting as the control method.

Other methods that are sometimes suggested include feeding suet to woodpeckers in the hope of discouraging damage. Placing nest boxes on nearby buildings, poles, or trees has also been advised, but there is no good information on whether these reduce the problem. They may, in fact, be attractants, leading to an increase in woodpecker numbers.

MONITORING GUIDELINES

Woodpeckers, like many other birds, are so visible that little specific monitoring information is needed. They may be heard pecking and drumming even before they are seen. Hearing their activity over several consecutive days provides a clue that a visual inspection is warranted. Vacation homes in forested areas should be checked for damage several times during the spring and summer.

Mammals

FIGURE 37.

Bats may roost in buildings, causing odors and harboring pests and diseases.

A variety of mammals can, at times, conflict with human interests and become pests. House mice, Norway and roof rats, and bats are the primary invaders of homes, raising health issues and potentially damaging property. Meadow voles, pocket gophers, ground squirrels, tree squirrels, rabbits, and deer are in the forefront of animals notorious for damaging gardens. Major nuisance problems develop as raccoons, opossums, and skunks frequent the garden and take up residence, creating health issues, damaging structures and plants, and fostering unpleasant encounters between pets and wildlife.

BATS

Bats (order Chiroptera) are relatively small flying mammals. The bats found in California feed on flying insects and are considered an important part of the ecological community. In most cases, bats do not cause problems for homeowners or gardeners. In fact, because of their nocturnal habits, they are often not seen, even though they may be present. The primary problems are associated with bats roosting in buildings and the potential transmission of diseases. Of the 24 species of bats identified in California, 5 form colonies or roosts in structures, particularly in older buildings with many openings and gaps through which they can enter (table 3).

Most bats eat insects and roost in tree foliage and cavities, under loose bark, and in caves and crevices. Some bats roost in buildings during warm months and hibernate elsewhere during winter (fig. 37). In spring, females form maternity colonies to bear and rear young. Males tend to be more solitary at this time and roost away from the females. Young, flightless bats stay in the roost at night, while the females forage. By mid-August, the young bats are flying and males may

TABLE 3.

Five species of bats that commonly form colonies or roosts in man-made structures in California

NAME	WINGSPREAD	DESCRIPTION
big brown bat (*Eptesicus fuscus*)	13–14 in (33.0–35.6 cm)	One of the largest bats found in buildings. Most are copper-colored. Each hair is bicolored: the basal half is blackish, the outer half brown.
little brown myotis (*Myotis lucifugus*)	8.9–10.8 in (22.6–27.4 cm)	Fur is dense, fine, glossy, and rich brown in color. Ears and membranes are glossy dark brown. Of all small brown bat species, this is the one most often found in buildings.
Mexican free-tailed bat (*Tadarida brasiliensis*)	11.3–13 in (28.7–33.0 cm)	A rather small bat with long, narrow wings, best identified by tail, which extends well beyond tail membrane.
pallid bat (*Antrozous pallidus*)	13–14 in (33.0–35.6 cm)	A large bat with big eyes, ears, and broad wings. Piglike snout is distinctive. Hairs above are light yellow and tipped with brown or gray. Underparts are pale creamy color. Membranes tan.
Yuma myotis (*Myotis yumanensis*)	8.7 in (22.1 cm)	Light tan to dark brown; under parts whitish to buff. Membranes darker than body.

also join the colony. As the weather cools and insect numbers decrease, bats usually migrate to preferred hibernation roosts for winter or to warmer areas, such as Southern California or the San Francisco Bay Area, where insects are more active in winter. Occasionally, bats hibernate in buildings. In spring and fall, migrating bats may temporarily roost in buildings as they move through an area.

Bats may create disturbances by squeaking and scratching in attics, walls, and chimneys. Their fecal droppings and urine accumulate beneath roosts, creating odors, and sometimes these seep through cracks, causing stains on ceilings and walls. In addition, bat feces may attract insects.

It is estimated that one in every thousand bats is infected with rabies, creating a potential threat to humans. Exposure usually occurs when sick bats are handled. Fortunately, bats that live in buildings rarely become aggressive but instead develop a paralytic form of the disease in which they become lethargic. They will bite in self-defense, however, and any bat bite must be treated as a possible rabies exposure. Because most human exposures occur from bites, never pick up or handle a sick or dying bat or do anything that will scatter sick, dead, or disabled bats where contact with people or pets may occur. If rabies is suspected, contact your local public health department for help.

Bats for Insect Control

Since bats eat flying insects, many have suggest that they can serve as natural control agents for mosquitoes and other pest insects. While studies have shown that they can have an impact on the insect population level, it is unlikely that having them around structures significantly reduces the number of insects in that area.

LEGAL RESTRAINTS OF CONTROL

No toxicants or chemical repellents are registered in California for control of bats.

CONTROL METHODS

Detecting Bats

The only permanent way to prevent bats from roosting in buildings is to physically exclude their entry. The first step is to inspect the building for possible entry and exit points for bats. A building in poor repair may have many entry points. Bats can squeeze through openings as small as ⅜ inch (9 mm). Look for loose flashing, vents, shingles, or siding; openings under eaves, cornices, louvers, and doors; and cracks around windows, chimneys, outlet boxes, and where pipes or electrical wiring enter the structure. Droppings under openings, smudges around holes, and odors are helpful clues. During daylight, you can sometimes detect openings when light shines through them into a dark attic. Roosting sites inside structures include attics, within walls, inside chimneys, or behind shutters.

Conduct two inspections of the building if you believe bats are present, one during the day and another at night. The daytime inspection should include searching for possible entrances and exits from the exterior and from roosting locations in the building, as well as searching for roosting colonies. The nighttime inspection should try to determine whether bats are actually leaving the building. Begin the inspection one-half hour before dusk and continue until about 1 hour after the first bat emerges. If no bats are seen after about 1 hour, bats may not be present or you cannot see emerging bats from your location. Locate two observers at opposite corners of the structure

FIGURE 38.

Install bird netting under eaves to prevent bats from entering.

so that each can view two roof lines at once. If the building has several wings, more assistants may be needed. Watch for emerging bats and note the openings they use. Bats seen emerging at evening from areas that were not identified during the day could indicate a roost in an inaccessible void. Counting the bats helps determine the size of the colony, but night-to-night occupancy can vary with migration and weather changes.

Bat-proofing Structures

Bat-proofing should be undertaken as soon as bats take up residence in a building. The best times for bat-proofing are in spring before young

are born or in fall after young bats are flying. Bat-proofing should not be done from about mid-May to mid-August if newborn, flightless bats are present, since closing entrances and exits either traps them inside or scatters them outside the roost site. Dying bats create unpleasant odors inside a building, and if the flightless young crawl away from the roost, they may bite children or pets trying to pick them up. If young bats are present, wait until they are flying, then bat-proof the building so they won't return the following year.

Bat-proofing often requires the use of ladders and other devices to get to the roost entry. Be careful, especially at night. Contact a professional if you are unsure about how to proceed. Begin bat-proofing by blocking and sealing openings in the early evening after the bats have departed. Seal all access points, including the one or two principal openings (fig. 38). Early the following evening, unplug the major openings to allow any remaining bats to escape. Reseal the opening(s) before any bats return. Repeat the routine if any bats are seen or heard within the structure. Watch the building for several evenings for any overlooked openings. If young bats are present, do not seal them in.

An alternative method done entirely by day is to plug all but the principal opening(s) and install on them a device that acts as a one-way valve (fig. 39). The valve consists of a rigid 2-inch (5-cm) diameter plastic pipe taped to a collapsible pliable tube. Plastic tarp or a similar material is suitable for the collapsible section. Attach the entire unit to the structure with the rigid pipe covering the last exit hole. Bats inside the roost can exit through the device but are unable to reenter the deformed, collapsed end of the pliable tube. In time, after all bats have left, remove the device and seal the hole permanently. If young bats are present, do not use this method. Wait until they leave the roost and then permanently seal the openings.

Bat-proofing Materials

Unlike rats and mice, bats cannot gnaw through wood and other common building materials, so a number of materials can be used to seal access points:

- caulking, putty, duct tape, silicone, and other cements for cracks, holes, and crevices
- self-expanding polyurethane foam for cracks, crevices, and corrugated and tile roofing
- weather stripping for around doors and windows
- door sweeps for under doors
- flashing where joints occur in a building
- hardware cloth (¼-inch mesh), window screening, and plastic bird netting (¼-inch mesh) for ventilators, louvers, and large openings
- insulation for blowing into wall and roof spaces
- rags, cotton, newspaper, and tape for temporary seals

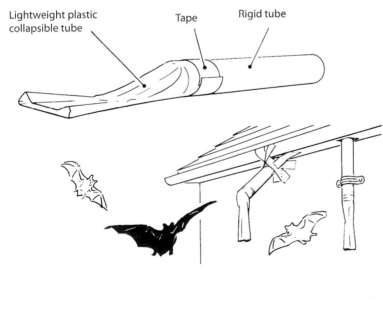

FIGURE 39.

Block all but one or two of the principal openings and install a one-way tube that allows bats to leave but prevents reentry.

Repelling Methods

Two methods applied singly or together may alter roost conditions sufficiently to cause bats to leave. Stringing electric lights for constant illumination of the roost has driven bats from some, but not all, roosts. Since bats roost in quiet and secluded areas, some believe that air movement makes the roost less hospitable. Breezes from electric fans aimed at bats have also been reported to be effective, although this method has not been tested. While they may be effective in some situations, these methods can also fail because the bats may be able to move into cracks and crevices to escape the light or breeze.

Temporary Outside Roosts

Bats in migration or male bats during the nursing season will temporarily roost in open areas under eaves, in porches, garages, and patios, or behind shutters. Tacking coarse fiberglass batting to the surface of these areas may discourage them.

Bats Inside Rooms

If you discover a bat inside your home, encourage it to leave by opening all the doors and windows. The bat will find its way out by detecting the fresh air movement. If it is dark outside, turn off all lights; otherwise, the bat may seek a dark refuge behind a curtain or wall hanging. As a last resort, catch the bat using an insect net or box. Avoid handling any bat unless you are wearing leather gloves.

Bat Houses (Artificial Roosts) for Alternative Roosting Sites

Artificial roosts have been suggested as dwellings for bats that have been excluded from buildings. Most people who have tried this approach have had difficulty in getting the bats to occupy these structures. As with supplemental feeding of wildlife, providing alternatives can sometime lead to increased overall numbers of the animals in the area. Clearly, some people like bats and want them around the garden. Artificial roosts may be the answer for this, but by themselves, they are not likely to prevent colonization of buildings.

Other Control Methods

Certain commercially available devices promise to repel bats or drive them away. Most of these devices generate ultrasonic sounds. Since bats hear and use ultrasonic sounds to navigate, some think that these unnatural sounds should frighten or otherwise disturb the bats. Unfortunately, there is little evidence that these devices work. There are no natural controls such as diseases or predators that control bats and keep them from roosting in structures.

MONITORING GUIDELINES

Bats are common throughout California. Some areas, especially where flying insects are common, may be more attractive and more likely to have bat roosts. Check structures in late winter and repair openings that bats could use to enter the building. If you are new to an area, ask neighbors and others about bats and their experiences with them in your area.

Deer

Most people enjoy seeing deer in the wild. Unfortunately, deer can be very destructive to gardens, orchards, and landscaped areas, particularly in foothill and coastal locations where nearby woodlands provide cover (fig. 40). Mule deer (*Odocoileus hemionus*) and blacktailed deer (*O. hemionus columbianus*), members of the Cervidae, or deer family, are the two subspecies common in California.

Mature deer are about 3 to 3½ feet (0.9 to 1.1 m) tall at the shoulder. They eat a variety of vegetation, including woody plants, grasses, and forbs (small broadleaved flowering plants) (fig. 41). They also consume shrubs, vines, garden vegetables, and fruit, nut, and ornamental trees (fig. 42). Deer trample plants and damage young trees and shrubs by rubbing their antlers on trunks and limbs (fig. 43). Because most deer feed in the late evening and very early morning, it is not always easy to observe them. A good way to determine their presence in the garden or orchard is to look for hoof prints. Deer hooves are split, pointed at the front and more rounded at the rear, and are about 2 to 3 inches (5 to 7.5 cm) long. Deer droppings are also a good indicator of their presence.

FIGURE 40.

Deer may be welcome visitors for a time, but they can become more destructive as time goes on.

FIGURE 41.

Deer eat a wide variety of vegetation and readily browse in areas such as lawns, parks, and cemeteries.

FIGURE 42.

Deer damage to camellias.

FIGURE 43.

An overpopulation of deer can severely damage landscape plantings, as shown at this home on the Monterey County coast.

LEGAL RESTRAINTS OF CONTROL

The California Fish and Game Code classifies deer as game animals. If you find them damaging property or crops, you may request a permit from your local game warden to shoot them, although this method is not generally recommended for deer around homes and gardens. Traps and poisons of any kind are illegal and cannot be used on deer.

CONTROL METHODS

Deterrents such as fences, barriers, frightening devices, and various repellents are recommended and can be used without a permit. Physical exclusion is by far the best and most reliable way to protect gardens, orchards, and ornamental plantings from deer.

Fencing

Properly built and maintained fencing is the most effective way to prevent deer damage (fig. 44). Deer normally will not jump a 6-foot (1.8-m) fence, but if chased or threatened they can clear an 8-foot (2.4-m) fence on level ground. Because of this, a

FIGURE 44.

Deer-proof fencing is the most effective way to prevent deer damage.

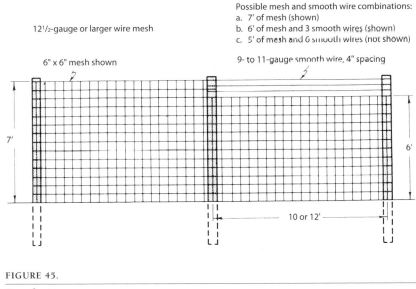

12½-gauge or larger wire mesh

6" x 6" mesh shown

Possible mesh and smooth wire combinations:
a. 7' of mesh (shown)
b. 6' of mesh and 3 smooth wires (shown)
c. 5' of mesh and 6 smooth wires (not shown)

9- to 11-gauge smooth wire, 4" spacing

7'

6'

10 or 12'

FIGURE 45.

Deer fencing.

fences are highly effective. Deer can crawl under or through a fence, so secure the fence close to the ground and repair any breaks. An extra strand of wire stretched along the ground below a conventional fence helps prevent deer from crawling under. Stake the wire or mesh firmly to the ground in any depressions between posts or fill the depressions with materials that will not deteriorate or wash away. If you need to economize, two or more strands of 9- or 10-gauge smooth wire spaced 4 to 6 inches (10 to 15 cm) apart can be stretched above a 6-foot (1.8-m) mesh. There is no advantage in using barbed wire for these top strands. The vertical stays or posts for mesh fences should be no more than 6 to 8 feet (1.8 to 2.4 m) apart to keep the wire tight. High-tensile wire fences are less expensive than wire mesh and can be very effective, although their construction requires special techniques. For more information on these types of fences, contact an agricultural fencing contractor or supplier.

A good deer fence works both ways. If an animal gets in, it can be difficult to get it out. A removable section in an uphill corner on sloping ground or, on level ground, a corner farthest from human activity can allow deer to be driven out of the fenced area.

Gates

A fence should have a gate that is the same height as the fence. Keep the weight of the gate to a minimum; a light, wood-framed, wire-mesh gate is often satisfactory. If you use factory-made aluminum gates, bolt metal extensions on them and stretch mesh wire over them to add height. Sink a wooden base or concrete apron in the ground below the gate to make a uniform sill to prevent deer from working their way under the gate.

Converting an existing fence

To make an existing fence deer-proof, attach uprights vertically or at an

7- or 8-foot (2.1- to 2.4-m) fence is recommended, especially in the Sierra Nevada mountain areas where larger deer are found (fig. 45). On sloping ground, you may need to build fences 10 to 11 feet (3.0 to 3.4 m) tall to guard against deer jumping down the slope.

The kind of fence you build depends on the cost, terrain, and your needs. High-tensile wire and woven mesh angle sloping away from the protected area (fig. 46). Attach wire mesh or smooth wires with no more than 4 to 6 inches (10 to 15 cm) of horizontal spacing between them. Most fences can be made deer-proof by extending their height 3 to 4 feet (0.9 to 1.2 m), provided that the lower portion is well-constructed and fits tightly against the ground. An often-unrecognized fact is that deer are more likely to crawl under or through a fence than to jump over it.

Electric fences

Standard electric fences used for livestock have not proved to be very effective for deer control in California. However, the New Zealand–type electric fence, built specifically for deer, with its high-tensile-strength wire and more intense charge, may be effective. One addition that can improve an electric fence for controlling deer is to attach a hot wire near the ground to prevent them from crawling under the fence. The New Zealand–type fence is best constructed by an experienced professional fence contractor. Electric fences need constant monitoring because they can short-out when touched by vegetation and can stop working for various other reasons.

Maintaining fences

Deer fences must be checked regularly. Repair damaged wire, broken gates, soil washout, or any weakness in construction that would permit deer access. The job becomes increasingly difficult as fences age and become vulnerable to breakage.

Individual Plant Protectors

In many situations, protecting individual plants may be more practical and economical than fencing an entire area. For example, young fruit or nut trees in a home orchard can be individually fenced until primary branches grow above the deer's reach, usually 5 to 7 feet (1.5 to 2.1 m). Poultry wire, heavy woven wire, or strong plastic netting can be attached to two stakes to form a circle around the tree (fig. 47). Plastic trunk protectors are especially useful for young vines and trees (fig. 48). Inspect individual protectors regularly because they can restrict plant growth. In addition, take care to ensure that the protector itself doesn't damage the vine or tree by causing an accumulation of excess heat or moisture.

Using Electric Fences

- [ ] Check with local authorities to see whether an electric fence is permissible in your area. Some cities or communities may prohibit them.

- [ ] Always use a commercially produced charger that is recommended for your proposed type of fence. These chargers are generally sold to gardeners or landscapers through garden supply catalog or retail sales outlets.

- [ ] Commercial fence chargers produce high voltages at very low amperages, which cause a significant shock but not with enough power to result in death.

- [ ] Never attempt to electrify a fence yourself without the use of an appropriate fence charger. This can be extremely dangerous and even fatal.

- [ ] Control the fence charger with a timer so it will be on only when needed.

- [ ] Post signs to alert people to the existence of an electric fence. Hang the signs on the fence or attach them to a post.

- [ ] Do not set up an electric fence if there is a chance that children may come into contact with it.

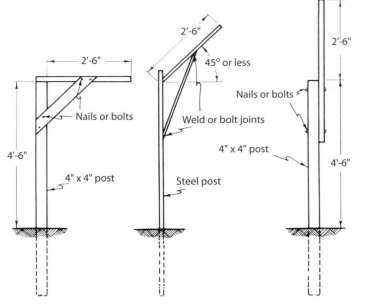

FIGURE 46.

Converting a common upright fence into a deer fence. Angled fence additions may pose some legal issues if the projections go over a property line.

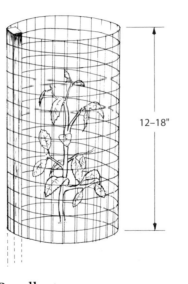

FIGURE 47.

A wire cage made of 1- or 2-inch mesh can protect an individual plant from deer.

Repellents

Various chemical repellents are marketed for reducing or preventing deer damage to trees, vines, and ornamentals, although their effectiveness in most situations is not very good or long-lasting. Deer repellents impart objectionable odors or tastes. Most are not allowed on food crops, so if that is the intended use, make sure the repellent is registered for that purpose. When deer are hungry and a garden area contains highly preferred foods, repellents are much less likely to be effective. Some repellents can injure trees or shrubs, especially new growth. If in doubt, test them on a single plant to make sure they are not phytotoxic (harmful to the plant).

Follow product label directions carefully when using deer repellents. Most repellents should be applied before damage occurs and must be reapplied frequently, especially after a rain, heavy dew, or sprinkler irrigation. Likewise, to be effective, repellents must usually be applied to new foliage as it develops. Commercially available repellents that produce odors thought to frighten or repel deer from an area include human hair, soap bars with an intense aroma, and mountain lion urine or other types of predator odors. Although these substances may repel deer for a day or two, they have not proved to satisfactorily protect gardens from deer damage in California.

Frightening and Other Control Methods

Deer rapidly adjust to noisemaking devices such as propane cannons and electronic alarms, making them ineffective. This is particularly true in areas where deer have frequent human contact. Not only are these devices ineffective, they can disturb neighbors, pets, livestock, and other animals.

Since deer can travel great distances to seek food and shelter, modifying their habitat to make it less desirable is usually impractical. Planting less-preferred plants in your garden or working together with neighbors to plant these plants over large areas might be effective in reducing deer numbers in a given area. Garden and landscape trees, shrubs, and vines often provide highly attractive browse, especially when new foliage is forming. Planting alternative attractive foods away from the garden does not prevent damage to more valued plants and may make the area more attractive to deer.

Deer, like all animals, have certain food aversions. You can often take

FIGURE 48.

FIGURE 48.

Install exclusion cylinders around individual trees to protect them from deer, rabbits, and other vertebrate pests.

advantage of this by planting deer-resistant ornamental plants. Many of the most resistant plants, such as oleander, are poisonous, either at all times or at certain stages of growth. The plant preferences of deer may vary depending on the time of year and where your garden is located. This is why one gardener may find that some ornamentals are resistant to deer while other gardeners say that deer love them. Repellency to deer is also related to the availability of other food. If there is a surplus of attractive native forage, ornamental plantings may be largely untouched. If the naturally occurring food supply is low, browsing pressure increases on domestic gardens. Under extreme food shortage, few plant species are totally resistant to deer. A large population of deer increases competition for forage, and deer may eat normally unpalatable plants.

Several lists of deer-resistant plants have been published. One of the most useful can be found in the *Sunset Western Garden Book* (Brenzel et al. 2000). These lists should be used as a general guide. Local nurseries or other gardeners may have information specific to your area, and landscaping or gardening catalogs may also designate deer-resistant plants.

MONITORING GUIDELINES

The first step to preventing damage from deer is to know whether they are in or around your garden. Although deer are large and easily seen, their nocturnal habits may make it necessary to check the garden at night with a flashlight. Also look for physical signs of deer such as tracks, droppings, trails, and damage to foliage from deer browsing. Because a few deer can do a lot of damage to a garden or landscaped area, take action when deer signs are first detected. If you know deer have caused problems nearby, consider using exclusion methods such as fences before damage occurs.

Deer Mice

Deer mice (*Peromyscus maniculatus*) are one of a very large group of species and subspecies of the genus *Peromyscus* that are widely distributed throughout the United States. As a group they are often referred to as white-footed mice. Six species of white-footed mice thrive in California, and of these the deer mouse is found most widely throughout the state, with the denser populations generally found in or near forested or wooded areas. The other species are more limited in distribution, preferring chaparral, piñon-juniper habitat, rocky canyons, and similar environments.

The color of deer mice varies between and within the species, but almost all have white underparts, belly, legs, and feet, contrasted by the upper parts, sides, and back, which are very dark to light brown (fig. 49). Large, prominent eyes, large ears, and a long bicolored tail about the length of the body characterize this entire group (fig. 50). This distinctly bicolored tail, white on bottom and dark on top, makes it easy to distinguish deer mice from the somewhat smaller and shorter house mouse.

Deer mice are essentially nocturnal and do not hibernate, but they may hole up for a few days in severe weather. For their size they have a large home range of up to 4 acres (1.6 ha). They readily seek out and eat conifer seeds, nuts, acorns, and fungi. Seeds from a wide variety of plants, depending on the locality, are consumed, along with a number of insects. As predominately seed, fungi, and insect feeders, they seldom consume grasses, forbs, bark, or leaves, as do the meadow voles. They have a great propensity to collect and hoard seeds for future consumption.

FIGURE 49.

Deer mouse. Note white feet and white underbelly.

Deer mice can be very prolific, producing two or more litters annually. The young are born at any time of the year but mostly during the spring or summer. The reproductive rate seems to depend on the abundance of the natural food supply, which often depends on favorable weather. Although not noticeably cyclic, their populations fluctuate markedly from year to year, and it is not uncommon for populations to jump from a few to as many as 20 to 25 per acre (about 50 to 60 per ha). A population of 15 or more per acre (37 per ha) is considered high.

Deer mice nest in secluded places such as rotting logs or stumps, under buildings, among rocks, and in burrows. Trees are also used for nesting, as are various locations in an unoccupied dwelling, such as a kitchen cupboard, dresser drawer, or stuffed chair. Litter size ranges from 3 to 6, and the females reach reproductive maturity at about 6 weeks of age. Adults rarely live more than about 2 years in the wild.

Except in areas of forest regeneration, deer mice are generally considered a pest of limited scope and significance, invading mountain cabins or other vacation facilities that remain unoccupied for a lengthy period. In 1993 the association of deer mice with the deadly hantavirus has brought them into greater focus, and they have taken on an increased importance because of this disease.

HEALTH IMPORTANCE

While deer mice have long been implicated in cases of Rocky Mountain spotted fever, it has only been in the last 10 years or so that they have been linked to the hantavirus. People can be infected by inhaling airborne particles of urine, droppings, or saliva from infected rodents; the virus may also be spread by touching the nose, mouth, or eyes after handling infected rodents, their nests, or droppings. Infection with the virus causes hantavirus pulmonary syndrome (HPS), a rare but serious disease that is fatal to about 50 percent of those who contract it. Most cases of HPS have been related to deer mice; however, the virus is not limited to this mouse and has been found in some other native rodents as well.

Hantavirus Precautions

It is highly critical that people avoid working or sleeping in enclosed spaces infested with deer mice or other rodents. Before occupying a vacation cabin or associated outbuildings, open the doors and windows to air out the room for at least 30 minutes if there is any indication that deer mice may have lived there. Where possible, use an electric fan to assist in the process. To minimize stirring up dust that carries the virus, do not vacuum or sweep floors before mopping. Wear vinyl or latex gloves and mop floors once or twice with a solution of water, detergent, and a commercial disinfectant. Carpets should be shampooed or commercially steam-cleaned. Clean counters, stoves, cabinets, drawers, and other surfaces by washing thoroughly with a solution identical to that used for mopping. A hypochlorite solution prepared by mixing 12 fluid ounces of household bleach in 1 gallon (400 ml in 4 l) of water may be used in place of commercial disinfectant. Remember, if using this 10 percent bleach solution, avoid spilling the mixture on clothing or other items that may be damaged. During the cleanup process, wearing a cloth or paper breathing mask offers some protection and is better than no protection at all; but only an approved respirator equipped with HEPA filters offers total respiratory protection.

Contact the Center for Disease Control (CDC) Hotline for the latest recommendations prior to cleaning

FIGURE 50.

Deer mouse. Note the characteristic large eyes and ears.

CONTROL METHODS

Deer mice are seldom a significant pest in homes and gardens, except in forested or wooded areas where they are now more of a health threat than a damage or economic threat. Control of deer mice in residences is not unlike that used for house mice (see pages 90–96). Habitat modification and exclusion are emphasized, with trapping and toxic baits offered for reduction and control. The value of exclusion, along with a recognition of the health hazards posed by these rodents, cannot be overstressed.

Habitat Modification

Because deer mice have a large home range, sometimes up to 4 acres (1.6 ha), habitat modification is not easily attained since the mice may be coming from areas beyond your control. You can, however, reduce nesting sites and create more open space, which makes the mice more susceptible to predation. In general, make the area less hospitable by eliminating weedy areas by clearing or mowing in much the same manner as discussed for meadow voles (see page 57). Clearing or cutting back brush not only reduces the fire hazard but also reduces deer mouse harborage as well. Brush removal, especially along paths and trails, also helps prevent ticks from attaching themselves to passersby. Clean up fallen trees and brush piles and thin out dense layers of duff beneath trees. You need not remove all of the duff: leave a thin layer to prevent erosion and prevent annual weeds from growing and providing habitat favorable to deer mice. Where possible, move wood stacks at least 20 feet (6 m) away from a house and try to keep a clean, clear area of ground area 2 feet (0.6 m) wide all around the house to slow the possible entry of deer mice or other rodents. This clear area also aids in finding entry holes that need plugging while conducting rodent exclusion efforts.

areas that have been infested with deer mice or other native rodents. These recommendations may also be found on the CDC hantavirus Web site at http://www.cdc.gov/ncidod/diseases/hanta/hps/index.htm.

If the control and cleanup of deer mouse infestation seems too overwhelming, it may be best to hire a licensed pest control operator who is trained and equipped to handle the situation.

LEGAL RESTRAINTS OF CONTROL

The California Fish and Game Code classifies deer mice as nongame mammals. Nongame mammals that are found to be injuring or threatening crops or other property may be controlled at any time or in any legal manner by the owner or tenant of the premises.

Exclusion

The most successful and permanent method of control in a residence or vacation cabin is to make the building rodent-proof. Seal cracks and openings in the foundation and any opening where water pipes, power or cable lines, sewer pipes, and air vents may enter. No hole larger than ¼ inch (6.5 mm) should be left unsealed, just as would be done to exclude house mice. Make sure that doors fit tightly at the bottom and install appropriate seals and weather stripping where needed. Because deer mice are also excellent climbers, openings above ground level must also be plugged. Deer mice often gain entry through fireplace chimneys, so install chimney screens (spark arrestors) of a mesh size that will exclude deer mice. Making a home completely mouse-proof is not easy and may be impossible to achieve in some mountain cabins and vacation residences located in forested areas, but with fewer openings available there is less chance of entry.

When leaving a vacation home or part-time home for a period of a month or more, store all foodstuffs in rodent-proof containers. This should also include food for pets, wild birds, and chipmunks.

Excluding deer mice using fencing is impractical because they are good climbers. If deer mice dig up garden seeds such as sunflower, corn, or pumpkin after planting, cover the rows with ¼-inch mesh wire until the seedlings are a few inches tall. Deer mice are interested only in seeds and insects as food, not the plants. If deer mice are climbing trees to feed on almond or other nut crops, place metal bands around the tree several feet above ground to prevent access.

Trapping

Deer mice found in or immediately around buildings can be trapped with ordinary mouse snap traps. Peanut butter or peanut butter mixed with dry oatmeal breakfast cereal works well as a bait. A dozen or more traps may be needed to decisively bring a high population under control. Keep a few traps set at all times, even after control has been achieved, to prevent reinvasion or resurgence of the mouse population. Wear vinyl or latex gloves when setting traps and removing carcasses from traps. As a precaution against hantavirus, spray 1 percent disinfectant consisting of 3 tablespoons of laundry bleach in 1 gallon (40 ml in 4 l) of water plus a little detergent; a spritz bottle works well. Seal carcasses in a bag and then put the bag into another bag (double bagging) before discarding. Some people feel safer discarding the trap along with the dead mouse. Keep trapped deer mice at arm's length, away from your breathing zone. Wash thoroughly when finished.

While deer mice can be live-captured in any of several available multiple-catch mouse traps, these traps should definitely not be used because of the greater potential exposure to hantavirus. These traps quickly become highly contaminated with mouse feces and urine and also present the added problem of how to euthanize the trapped mouse.

Glue Boards

For indoor use an alternative to traps is glue boards, just as used for house mice. These work on the same principle as sticky flypaper—when a mouse attempts to cross a glue board it gets stuck. For deer mice select the larger-sized glue boards sold to catch rats, as they are more effective for these mice. Locate glue boards in secluded areas along walls or in other places where mouse droppings are observed. Glue boards tend to lose their effectiveness in dusty areas, and extremes of temperature may affect the tackiness of the adhesive. While wearing gloves, place the glue board along with the trapped dead mouse in plastic bags (double bagging) and seal before discarding.

Toxic Bait

When a population becomes exceptionally high in spite of habitat management, toxic bait may be needed to achieve adequate control in a timely way. In general, the same rodenticide baits effective for house mice are also effective for deer mice. Some marketed anticoagulant baits containing chlorophacinone, diphacinone, or warfarin, for example, are labeled specifically to include deer mice in addition to rats and house mice. Anticoagulants interfere with an animal's blood clotting mechanism, eventually leading to death. They are generally effective only when consumed over a period of several days.

Anticoagulant baits are available in several forms: meals, whole grains, small pellets, and paraffinized baits of various sizes. While the smaller sized baits may be more readily eaten by the mice, their tendency to hoard this type of bait is enormous, and the use of the larger paraffinized type bait blocks may be preferred as they are too large to be easily carried off. You might wish to try some of both.

Anticoagulant baits are used or applied in bait boxes or by broadcast baiting. Bait boxes or stations can be homemade or purchased commercially in sizes designed for house mice or rats. Either size is suitable for deer mice and when properly placed and anchored will keep the bait confined and dry and will prevent nontarget animals from gaining access to the bait. To alert people, clearly label all bait containers with an appropriate warning.

With few exceptions, toxic baits should be limited to the exterior of homes or to outbuildings such as woodsheds, pump houses, and tool sheds, so that deer mice that die in inaccessible places will not emit an unpleasant persistent odor of decay. In an effort to control deer mice that may find their way inside, some vacation cabin owners apply toxic baits in several places indoors prior to leaving the premises vacant and unused for a few months. This is a very effective long-term solution, and the owners are willing to take the chance that dead mice will have desiccated before they return to the home. In this way, the deer mouse will be killed as it enters and feeds on the bait, never having a chance to cause significant contamination or to multiply indoors. In addition, or as an alternative, a dozen or more set traps can be left inside the home. Air out the home well before inhabiting.

In some situations, such as play yards, campgrounds, and other recreation areas, broadcast baiting may be the best solution to bring a high deer mouse population under control within a few weeks. The bait must be registered for deer mouse control and the label must state that broadcast application is permissible and must specify the rate of application. This is often the application method of choice to control problem deer mice in forestry and agricultural production.

Repellents

Commercially available rodent repellents designed to be applied outdoors as an area or barrier repellent have not proved to be sufficiently effective to justify the expense. Mothballs or moth crystals are sometimes used as a home remedy in chests of drawers in vacation cabins in an effort to repel deer mice, and some success has been reported with this technique. Foresters use repellents to treat tree seed destined for reforestation purposes, and seed treatments also prevent depredation by deer mice in certain agricultural plantings.

Biological Control

High populations of deer mice have been known to have a significant impact on certain forest insect pests by feeding, for example, on the pupae of the larch sawfly. In this sense, they may be serving as a biological control agent of this pest.

Deer mice and other members of the genus *Peromyscus* are among the most widespread and numerous rodents in California, and they serve as a food resource for a large number of both avian and mammal predators. Their greatest predators are owls, weasels, skunks, badgers, foxes, coyotes, bobcats, and snakes. Collectively, these predators may significantly reduce the deer mouse population, yet deer mice, even in the remotest areas, will continue to thrive and reach pest status.

MONITORING GUIDELINES

Once deer mice have been brought under control and excluded from a residence, a reinvasion will be fairly easy to detect by the presence of droppings, nests, and the often-visible remnants of feeding. However, a house mouse invasion rather than a return of deer mice cannot be ruled out, as the signs are all similar except for the lack of the musky odor common to house mice. Visual surveillance at night in the dark with a flashlight or trapping a specimen may be the only way to confirm the identity of a new infestation.

Monitoring deer mice outdoors is very difficult, as they are small, nocturnal, and rarely observed. They do not produce visible runways, their droppings are hard to find, and they rarely produce burrows although they are capable of doing so. Even when present, burrow holes are difficult to locate. Nests are built in secluded sites, and so few are usually found that you cannot use them to determine the size of an infestation. Trapping is left as the most important tool for estimating deer mouse populations and the changes in populations from year to year.

GROUND SQUIRRELS

Ground squirrels (*Spermophilus* spp.), members of the Sciuridae, or squirrel family, inhabit most areas of California and are often found around buildings, gardens, and industrial sites, as well as along roads, in parks, at the edge of wooded areas, and in other natural environments. This chapter provides information about controlling relatively small numbers of ground squirrels in the home garden. When ground squirrel populations become large or are spread over agricultural areas or rangeland, control methods other than those discussed here may be more practical or economical.

Ground squirrels damage many food-bearing and ornamental plants. Particularly vulnerable are all types of grains and fruits and nuts such as almonds, apples, apricots, peaches, pistachios, plums, oranges, tomatoes, and walnuts (figs. 51–52). Ground squirrels also eat certain vegetables and field crops at the seedling stage. They damage young shrubs, vines, and trees by gnawing bark, girdling trunks, eating twigs and leaves, and burrowing around roots. Ground squirrels even gnaw surface-type plastic irrigation pipe (fig. 53).

Ground squirrels live in underground burrows. In the process of digging burrows, they excavate large amounts of soil that can bury and kill grasses or other small plants. Burrows and mounds make it difficult to irrigate and mow and

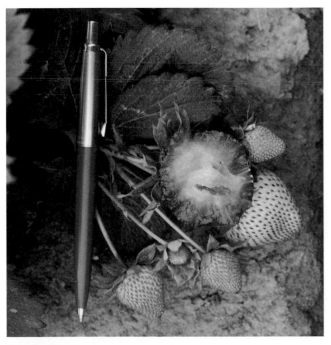

FIGURE 51.

Ground squirrel damage to strawberries.

FIGURE 52.

Ground squirrels remove the meat from nuts such as almonds, shown here, leaving the husks and hulls.

present a hazard to people, livestock, and machinery. Ground squirrels frequently burrow around trees and shrubs, gnawing the roots and causing excessive aeration, which sometimes kills the plant. Burrows beneath buildings and other structures can cause concrete foundations to crack and buildings to lean, requiring repair or replacement (fig. 54).

Ground squirrels can transmit diseases such as Rocky Mountain spotted fever and plague to humans, particularly when squirrel populations are dense. If you notice unusual numbers of dead squirrels or other rodents when no control has been undertaken, notify public health officials. Do not handle dead squirrels with your bare hands.

California has two main species of ground squirrels. The California ground squirrel (*Spermophilus beecheyi*) is found in most low-elevation areas except the Mojave Desert. The Belding or Oregon ground squirrel (*S. beldingi*) is found at higher elevations in the northeast counties and regions of the Sierra Nevada. The California ground squirrel is larger, with a head and body from 9 to 11 inches (23 to 28 cm) long and a somewhat bushy tail. The Belding ground squirrel's head and body measures 8 to 9 inches (20.5 to 23 cm). It has a relatively short and flat-looking tail, about 2½ to 3 inches (6.5 to 7.5 cm) long.

FIGURE 53.

Gnaw marks made by ground squirrels on plastic irrigation line.

Ground squirrels live in a wide variety of natural habitats, but populations may be particularly dense in disturbed areas such as road or ditch banks, fencerows, around buildings, and in or bordering many crops. They usually avoid thick chaparral, dense woods, and wetland areas. They live in colonies that can contain 20 or more animals if left undisturbed. Much of their time is spent in underground burrows where they sleep, rest, rear young, store food, and escape danger.

Ground squirrels are active during the day and are easily seen, especially in warm weather from spring to fall. During winter months, most ground squirrels hibernate, but it is common for some young to remain active, particularly in areas where winters are not severe. Most adults go into summer hibernations (aestivation) for short periods during the hottest times of the year.

FIGURE 54.

Ground squirrels can burrow beneath concrete slab founda-tions, resulting in structural damage.

Ground squirrels reproduce once a year in the spring. Litter sizes vary, but 7 to 8 young are average. The young remain in the burrow about 6 weeks before they emerge to start feeding on vegetation.

Ground squirrels are primarily vegetarian. During early spring they eat green grasses and forbs. When the native vegetation begins to dry on the hillsides, squirrels' food preferences switch to weed seeds, grains, and acorns. In the fall they store seeds and nuts in their burrows and may carry off your entire backyard orchard nut crop. In gardens the squirrels' food preferences may differ. They eat a much wider variety of food including tomatoes, beans, lettuce, oranges, apples, apricots, and peaches. They are fond of many types of annual and perennial flowers as well. Ground squirrels are known to eat or gnaw bark from bushes and trees, but this is not common (fig. 55).

LEGAL RESTRAINTS OF CONTROL

The California Fish and Game Code classifies ground squirrels as nongame mammals. If ground squirrels threaten growing crops or other property of which you are the owner or tenant, you may control the squirrels using any legal means.

Ground squirrels should not be confused with tree squirrels (*Sciurus* and *Tamiasciurus* spp.), which are classified as game animals. Although ground squirrels can and do climb trees, the two species can usually be distinguished by their response to danger: frightened ground squirrels retreat to a burrow; tree squirrels climb a tree or high structure. Also, ground squirrels have relatively smaller tails in proportion to their bodies. For more information, see the chapter "Tree Squirrels."

FIGURE 55.

Bark damaged by ground squirrel gnawing.

CONTROL METHODS

Ground squirrels can be a serious pest, and it is unfortunate that the few nonlethal methods for their control are rarely effective. They can be excluded from buildings but a ground squirrel-proof fence that permanently protects a garden is difficult to construct because of the animals' climbing and digging ability. Several methods of lethal control have been developed, including trapping, burrow fumigants, and toxic baits, which are effective but require some persistence on the part of the user. Ground squirrels have a unique annual life cycle, which influences the effectiveness of lethal control measures (fig. 56).

Trapping

Several types of kill traps are available for ground squirrels. Most work best if placed on the ground a few feet in front of the burrow entrance. A sufficient number of traps, perhaps one for every 4 or 5 active burrow openings, must be set to decisively reduce the population within a few weeks. To increase their effectiveness, bait traps but do not set them for several days so the squirrels become accustomed to them. Once the squirrels are readily taking the bait, rebait and set the traps. Walnuts, almonds, oats, barley, melon rinds, and orange slices are attractive trap baits.

Live-catch traps are not recommended because of the problem of disposing of the live ground squirrel. Releasing the trapped animal on another property is illegal without a permit from the Fish and Game Department. To do so risks the spread of diseases and may create a pest problem wherever the squirrel is released.

Certain box-type gopher traps also make effective squirrel kill traps. They can be improved by modifications such as fastening the trap to a baseboard after removing the back, adding a wire bait compartment, or anchoring two modified traps back to back on the same base board (fig. 57). If a baseboard is not affixed to the trap, anchor the trap with a wire attached to a stake to prevent the trap and its catch from being carried away by a dog or other predator. See the chapter on tree squirrels for additional information.

An all-metal tunnel or tube trap is becoming more popular for kill-trapping ground squirrels (fig. 58). It is

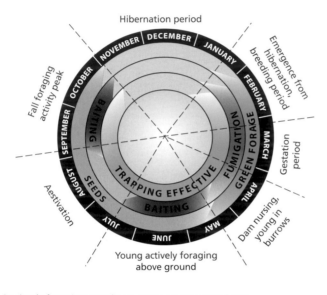

- ▨ Squirrels foraging mostly on green grasses and forbs.
- ▨ Squirrels foraging mostly on seeds.
- ▨ Trapping can be effective any time squirrels are active.
- ▨ Ideal time to fumigate burrows.
- ▧ Best times for baiting.
- ▨ Baiting marginally effective because of aestivation.

FIGURE 56.

Life cycle of the ground squirrel.

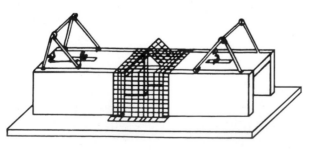

FIGURE 57.

An excellent ground squirrel trap can be made by fastening two modified box-type gopher traps back to back.

FIGURE 58.

The tunnel-type trap kills animals that pass through it.

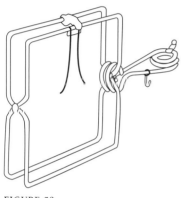

FIGURE 59.

Body-grip Conibear trap in set position.

FIGURE 60.

Conibear trap set in a trap box near a squirrel burrow entrance.

best set directly in the squirrel's trail and can be baited with grain such as oats or barley. These traps offer good protection for larger nontarget animals and are sturdy enough to be used in a horse pasture or around large domestic animals.

The Conibear 110 trap is also an effective ground squirrel kill trap (fig. 59). (Other manufacturers make similar traps sold under different trade names.) The trap has a catch opening approximately 4 inches by 4 inches

(10 cm by 10 cm) with a single spring. A more powerful version has two springs, one on either side. The wire trigger permits the trap to be used either baited or, when placed over the burrow entrance, without bait. It is best to set the trap directly in the burrow opening or where physical restrictions in the squirrel runway will direct the animal through the trap, tripping the trigger.

If squirrels are invading from someone else's property and you don't have access to the burrow, place the Conibear trap in one of several types of trap boxes at the edge of the property (fig. 60). A long trap box similar to figure 108 (page 81) provides greater protection to nontarget animals.

Baits are required in these boxes to entice the squirrel into the trap. Do not attach baits directly to the trigger; scatter them behind the trap.

Other ground squirrel traps are available but may have to be ordered from a trap supply firm. All squirrel kill traps have strong springs and are capable of killing animals of an equal size or injuring the fingers of a curious child. Do not place traps where they may pose a hazard to children, nontarget wildlife, pets, or poultry.

Fumigation

Ground squirrels can be killed in their burrows by several types of toxic gases, one of which requires a special permit from the local county agricultural commissioner. Follow all instructions on the product label. Fumigation is most effective in the spring or at other times when soil moisture is high. At those times, gas is contained within the burrow system and does not diffuse into small cracks that are often present in dry soil.

Ground squirrel burrows are quite large and can have several entrances. Treat and seal all entrances. Fumigation is not effective during periods of hibernation or aestivation because the squirrel plugs its burrow with soil. Plugs are not obvious when examining the burrow entrance.

The USDA produces a relatively safe and easy-to-use smoke/gas cartridge for fumigating burrowing rodents. The cartridge is a mixture of chemicals that, when ignited, produces a suffocating gas. Cartridges are available at many county agricultural commissioners' offices and can be used without a permit. Several commercially manufactured ignitable fumigation cartridges are also available at retail outlets. When using any cartridge-type fumigant, follow label instructions.

Use a smoke cartridge when fresh digging indicates the presence of an active ground squirrel burrow. Place the cartridge in the burrow opening and light the fuse. With a shovel handle or stick, push the lighted cartridge as far down the burrow as possible and quickly seal the opening with soil, tamping it down tightly. Seal connected burrows if smoke escapes from them. Larger burrow systems usually require two or more cartridges placed in the same or connecting burrow openings. After 24 hours, retreat reopened burrows.

Gases emitted from the cartridge occasionally flare up, creating a fire danger. Do not use smoke cartridges where a fire hazard exists, such as near buildings, dry grasses, or other flammable materials. Fumigation should never be used near or beneath buildings, as the gases produced are toxic to all animals.

Toxic Baits

Rodenticide baits are often used for controlling ground squirrels. Rodent baits are available over the counter, but ground squirrels must be specified on the pesticide label if they are to be used for this species. Some ground squirrel baits require a permit issued by the county agricultural commissioner. Gardeners or homeowners generally will not need to purchase or use enough bait to require a permit. However, check with the local agricultural commissioner's office if you have any questions. When using rodent baits or any other rodent control materials, follow label instructions carefully.

Cereal-based anticoagulant baits are recommended for controlling ground squirrels because they are effective and relatively safe to humans. Be sure the anticoagulants used are registered (labelled) for ground squirrels. Anticoagulants interfere with an animal's blood clotting mechanism, eventually leading to death. They are effective only when consumed in several feedings over several days. These features, as well as an effective antidote (Vitamin K_1) make anticoagulant baits relatively safe.

Anticoagulant baits can be applied in bait stations or by repeated spot or broadcast baiting. Bait stations or bait boxes are small structures that the squirrel must enter to eat the bait. They contain enough bait for repeated feedings and help keep children and pets from reaching the bait. Bait stations are the preferred baiting method around homes and other areas where children, pets, or poultry are present. Unless a bait label specifies otherwise, bait stations can be constructed from any durable material in a variety of designs. Tamper-resistant squirrel bait stations are commercially available. Bait stations generally must be labeled as a pesticide service container, and the label must include the name of the product, active ingredient, signal word ("Caution," "Danger," or "Warning"), and the party responsible for installing the station. If you have questions, contact your local agricultural commissioner.

The entrance hole(s) to a bait box or station for ground squirrels should be 3 inches (7.5 cm) across to allow squirrels access but not larger animals.

FIGURE 61.

Bait stations for ground squirrels can be made from plastic drainpipe. The half cap at the entrance confines the bait but allows squirrels to enter and feed.

Construct a lip to prevent bait from spilling out of the box when squirrels exit. Provide a lock on the box or devise some other method that makes it difficult for children to open the box. The bait box should be secured so that it cannot be turned over or easily removed. The self-feeding arrangement ensures that pests get a continuous supply of bait. A buried bait station with entrance tunnels is particularly useful in parks and other public areas. Buried bait stations are relatively permanent and can be constructed from a large valve-type box and two short sections of corrugated flexible plastic drainpipe 3 to 4 inches (7.5 to 10 cm) in diameter (fig. 61).

Place bait stations containing 1 to 5 pounds (0.45 to 2.27 kg) of bait in areas frequented by ground squirrels, for example, near runways or burrows. If ground squirrels live throughout an area, space the boxes at intervals of about 100 to 200 feet (30 to 60 m).

Initially, inspect bait boxes or stations daily and add bait as needed. Increase the amount of bait if all is eaten overnight. Fresh bait is important; replace old, moldy, or insect-infested bait. It may take a number of days before squirrels become accustomed to and enter the bait box. Stations with anticoagulant baits generally require 2 to 4 weeks or more to be effective, and they do not immediately affect feeding habits of squirrels. Continue baiting until all feeding ceases and no squirrels are observed. Pick up and safely dispose of unused bait upon completion of the control program. Anticoagulant baits used in large quantities or those obtained from county agricultural commissioners may require permits.

In situations where bait stations are not suitable, repeated spot-baiting with anticoagulant bait can effectively control ground squirrels over large areas. Follow label instructions. If spot-

Safeguarding Pets From Rodenticides

- ☐ Dogs become accidental victims of rodenticide poisoning more often than do cats.

- ☐ Dogs are less finicky eaters than cats and are more likely to consume cereal-based baits or chew on paraffin-type baits (bait blocks).

- ☐ Primary poisoning (consuming a toxic bait) is far more often the cause of poisoning in dogs than is secondary poisoning (consuming a poisoned animal).

- ☐ In some instances, both primary and secondary poisoning may be implicated.

- ☐ If you see your dog or cat feeding on rodent bait, seek a veterinarian's advice and provide the veterinarian with the type and name of the rodenticide involved. If you must take your pet to the veterinarian, take in the rodenticide box or packaging with you, if possible.

- ☐ Veterinarians are well aware that all rodenticides are not alike and will vary the treatment accordingly.

- ☐ If you are using a rodenticide on your property, keep an eye on your pets. Poisoned dogs and cats often become lethargic and may show signs of bleeding. Bloody feces or bleeding about the nose, mouth, or ears may be an early indication of anticoagulant rodenticide poisoning.

- ☐ Check bait placements or bait stations daily. If pets are gaining access to the bait, signs of this disturbance may be evident.

- ☐ If your pets are not confined to your property, they may be exposed to rodenticides elsewhere.

- ☐ If you are in doubt about your ability to safeguard your pets from poison baits, select an alternative method of control, such as exclusion or traps.

baiting or broadcast baiting is not specified on the product label, do not use this baiting method.

Anticoagulant baits have the same effect on nearly all warm-blooded animals, including birds. Cereal-based baits are attractive to some dogs and other nontarget animals, so take care to deny them access to the bait. Placing bait out of their reach, as in a bait box, can reduce danger to children and pets. Dead ground squirrels may contain some anticoagulant in their tissues. They should be buried or placed in plastic bags and discarded in the trash. Do not handle them with your bare hands. If a person or pet ingests anticoagulant bait, contact a physician or veterinarian immediately.

Ground squirrels are generally found in open areas, although they will use cover when available. Removing brush piles and debris not only makes an area less desirable to ground squirrels; it also makes detecting squirrels and their burrows easier, aids in monitoring the population, and improves access during control operations. After squirrels have been killed by trapping, burrow fumigation, or poison baits, invading squirrels readily reuse the empty burrows. This reoccupation can be slowed by filling in the openings of the vacated systems as completely as possible with soil and tamping them down. A single shovel of soil in the opening is usually not effective.

Biological Control

Many predators, including hawks, eagles, rattlesnakes, and coyotes, eat ground squirrels. In most cases, predators alone are not able to keep ground squirrel populations below the level at which they become pests. Predators can sometimes prevent ground squirrels from invading marginal habitats where cover is not abundant. Dogs may keep them from entering small areas, but they generally cannot control established squirrel populations.

MONITORING GUIDELINES

Once ground squirrel damage has been controlled, establish a system to monitor the area for reinfestation. Observe the area from a concealed spot during the morning hours, when squirrels are most active. Ground squirrels may move in from other areas and cause new damage within a short time. It is easier, less expensive, and less time-consuming to control a population before it builds up to the point where damage is significant.

Meadow Voles

Meadow voles (*Microtus* spp.) are represented by several similar species in California (fig. 62). Also known as meadow mice, they damage a wide range of plants by feeding and gnawing on trunks, roots, stems, and leaves (fig. 63). They are common in alfalfa fields, irrigated pastures, and some row crops (figs. 64–65). They also invade gardens, orchards, vineyards, and landscaped areas (figs. 66–67).

Meadow voles are small rodents in the family Crecitidae with stocky bodies, short legs and tails, and small rounded ears. Their long, coarse fur is blackish-brown to grayish-brown. When fully grown, they are 4 to 5 inches (10 to 12.5 cm) long. They are larger than a house mouse but smaller than a rat. Meadow voles are active night and day, all year long, and are found in areas with dense, grassy ground cover. They are relatively poor climbers and do not usually enter buildings. They dig short, shallow burrows with numerous openings about 2 inches (5 cm) across and make underground nests of grass, stems, and leaves. The peak breeding period is in spring, although second and third litters may occur up until the fall. Litters average 4 young.

Meadow vole numbers fluctuate dramatically from time to time; under favorable conditions their populations increase rapidly. Most damage caused by meadow voles occurs around homes and gardens during these cycles of rapid population increases and high numbers. In the low portion of the cycle, no problem may exist for years, and suddenly in the short span of a few months, the population explodes, catching gardeners by surprise. During these peak periods females may produce 8 or more litters per year, with the young maturing at less than 6 weeks of age. Turf is particularly vulnerable to damage when voles are numerous, but ornamentals shrubs and trees are susceptible as well.

FIGURE 62.

Meadow vole.

FIGURE 63.

Meadow vole damage to tree bark.

FIGURE 64.

Meadow vole damage to Brussels sprouts.

FIGURE 65.

Meadow vole damage to artichoke plant.

FIGURE 66.

Meadow vole damage to turf.

LEGAL RESTRAINTS OF CONTROL

The California Fish and Game Code classifies meadow voles as nongame mammals. If you find meadow voles threatening growing crops or other property of which you are the owner or tenant, you may control them using any legal means.

CONTROL METHODS

Preventing meadow vole damage usually requires a management program that keeps down the vole population in the area. In a small garden or backyard orchard, the first step is to make the area less supportive of vole habitation by removing extraneous vegetative cover, such as weedy forbs and grasses. Removing cover also makes detecting voles and other rodents easier. Since this is not always practical or desirable in landscaped areas, a program to exclude or control the vole population may be necessary. Because these animals can severely damage ornamental and garden plants, and because they reproduce rapidly, initiate a program of habitat modification or population reduction or both before their numbers explode.

Habitat Modification

Habitat modification is particularly effective in deterring voles. Grassy weeds, heavy mulch, and other dense covers encourage meadow voles by providing food and protection from predators and other environmental stresses. If you remove this protection, the area will be much less suitable to voles, and they may never build up to damaging levels. Clearing grassy areas adjacent to gardens can help prevent damage because it reduces the cover from which voles invade. Weed-free strips can serve as buffers around areas to be protected, but this is often not practical in a small garden. The wider the cleared strip, the less apt meadow voles will be to cross it and become established in gardens. A minimum width of 15 feet (4.5 m) is recommended, but even that might not be enough when vole numbers are high. Clearing vegetation about 2 feet (0.6 m) from young trees or vines reduces damage because voles shy away from feeding in the open. Voles often damage plants beneath thick mulches or bark chips laid over plastic sheeting, which is sometimes used around ornamental plantings.

Exclusion

Plastic, wire, or metal barriers that are at least 1 foot (0.3 m) high (2 feet, or 0.6 m, is preferred) with a mesh size of ¼ inch (6.5 mm) or less excludes meadow voles from landscape and garden areas. Meadow voles rarely climb these barriers, but they may dig beneath them. Bury the bottom edge 6 to 10 inches (15 to 25.5 cm). Individual plastic or hardware cloth cylinders surrounding the trunks can protect young trees, vines, and ornamentals. The bottom of these devices must be buried at least 6 inches (15 cm) in the soil to prevent voles from gaining access to the plant, and the cylinders must be supported so that they cannot be pushed over or pressed against the trunk.

Repellents

Several commercial repellents are registered for protecting plants from meadow voles, although they have not been proven to be effective or practical in California. Voles usually damage plants at or just beneath the soil surface, making adequate coverage with repellents difficult or impossible. Because rain, sprinklers, or even heavy dew often washes repellents away, you

FIGURE 67.

Meadow vole girdling has caused these shrubs to turn brown.

FIGURE 68.

Set meadow vole traps perpendicular to runway.

garden, 24 to 48 traps is probably the minimum number required, and 100 or more may be needed for larger areas. Examine traps daily. Remove and bury dead voles or place them in plastic bags in the trash. Do not handle voles without wearing plastic or rubber gloves.

Toxic Bait

When meadow voles are very numerous or when damage occurs over large areas, you may need to use toxic baits to achieve adequate control. If you use poison baits, follow the product label carefully and take care to ensure the safety of children, pets, and nontarget animals. Use only baits registered for voles.

Anticoagulant baits are slow-acting and must be consumed over a period of several days to be effective. Pelleted or whole grain baits are commonly recommended. Because the pest must feed on most anticoagulant baits over a period of several days, the bait must be available until the vole population is controlled. As with trapping, bait placement is very important. Place it in runways, next to burrows, or in burrow openings so voles will find it during their normal travel (fig. 69). If the rodenticide label allows it to be broadcast, do so, following the label instructions. Reapply according to the label. Read and follow the label carefully. These baits are toxic to most animals, so care must be taken to prevent access to them by nontarget wildlife. Placing baits in small stations, such as a 1-foot (0.3-m) section of a 2-inch (5-cm) plastic pipe, offers some safeguard to nontarget species and protects bait from the elements. When labeled for use against voles, anticoagulant moisture-resistant paraffin bait blocks can also be used. Place paraffin block or tube stations directly in runways or near burrow openings. Exposed bait blocks can present a hazard to dogs if they pick

must reapply them to give continued protection. Repellents should not be applied to food crops unless this use is specified on the product label.

Trapping

When vole numbers are low or when the population is concentrated in a small area, trapping may be an effective control method. The simple mouse trap with a wooden base is commonly used; newer models with an enlarged plastic treadle are best. Peanut butter, oatmeal, or apple slices make excellent baits for meadow voles. Often, no bait is needed because voles trigger traps as they pass over them.

Trap placement is crucial. Meadow voles seldom stray far from their usual travel trails or runways, so set traps along these routes. Look for nests, burrow openings, and runways in grass or mulch in or near the garden. To increase the number of voles trapped, place baited traps in these runways at a right angle with the trigger directly in the path of the vole (fig. 68).

Traps must be set in sufficient numbers to be effective. For a small them up and chew on them. Replace baits as they are eaten and remove those that remain when feeding stops. Rat and mouse baits available over the counter are not registered for voles and should not be used for their control.

Baits containing zinc phosphide are available for use by certified pesticide applicators. While not commonly used around homes and gardens, zinc phosphide can be used if the vole population is high and occupies a large area. In these situations, it may be prudent to hire an experienced wildlife pest control operator.

Biological Control

Voles are one of the most numerous animals in California and other states across the nation. They are a food resource for a wide range of animals, including hawks, owls, seagulls, crows, weasels, skunks, foxes, coyotes, rattlesnakes, and gopher snakes. Voles are a particular favorite of barn owls, which can be encouraged to inhabit an area by constructing suitable nest boxes. However, even if barn owls nest nearby, there is no assurance that they will feed on voles from your garden.

In fact, there is little evidence that owls have any measurable effect on vole populations. Although predators may kill many voles, they cannot keep vole populations in a garden below damaging levels.

Dogs and cats that are good hunters may reduce the invasion of voles into your garden or slow their buildup, but once voles are well established, they become too numerous for pets to effect any major control.

MONITORING GUIDELINES

To detect the presence of voles, look for fresh trails or runways in the grass, as well as burrow openings, droppings, and grass clippings as evidence of feeding. Routinely monitor the garden and surrounding area. Pay particular attention to adjacent areas that have dense, low-growing vegetation, especially grasses, because voles can build up in these areas and invade the garden. After vole populations peak, they generally subside even if no control has taken place. A low population may exist for 4 to 8 years before another resurgence.

FIGURE 69.

Place toxic bait in meadow vole runway or next to burrow opening.

MOLES

Moles (*Scapanus* spp.) are small insect-eating mammals that belong to the order Insectivora and the family Talpidae; they are not rodents, although they may resemble pocket gophers in some of their characteristics. In California, the broad-footed mole (*S. latimanus*) is the main species (fig. 70). It inhabits the Sierra Nevada and Coast Range mountains and foothills, as well as the entire coastal zone. Moles are not generally found in dry southeastern regions of the state or in much of the Central Valley except for moister areas such as river banks with soil rich in humus. Moles live almost entirely underground in a vast network of interconnecting tunnels. They frequently create shallow tunnels just below the surface where they capture worms, insects, and other invertebrates. They can eat roots, bulbs, and other plant material, but the problem is generally their burrowing, which dislodges plants and dries out their roots. In lawn areas the mounds and ridges caused by their burrowing are unsightly and disfiguring.

Broad-footed moles are 5 to 6 inches (12.5 to 15 cm) long and have cylindrical bodies with slender, pointed snouts and short, bare, or sparsely haired tails. Their limbs are short and spadelike. Their eyes are poorly developed and their ears are not visible. The fur is short, dense, and velvety. Moles have one litter of 3 to 4 young during early spring.

The volcano-shaped mounds formed by moles are pushed up from a tunnel in the center of the mound (figs. 71–72). The excavated soil may be in small chunks, and single mounds often form a line over the runway connecting them. The main runways or tunnels are usually about 2 inches (5 cm) in diameter and from 8 to 12 inches (20.5 to 30.5 cm) below the surface and are used repeatedly. Surface-feeding burrows appear as ridges that the mole pushes up by forcing its way through the soil and may be abandoned after a few uses (fig. 73). Moles are active throughout the year, although

FIGURE 70.

Broad-footed mole.

FIGURE 71.

Side view of a mole mound.

surface activity slows or is absent during periods of extreme wetness, cold, heat, or drought.

LEGAL RESTRAINTS OF CONTROL

The California Fish and Game Code classifies moles as nongame mammals. If you find moles threatening growing crops or other property of which you are the owner or tenant, you may control the moles using any legal means.

CONTROL METHODS

Moles can cause significant problems in landscape or garden areas, especially in turf. Several methods of control are available, but, since no easy method has proved successful, it may be necessary to use a combination of techniques.

Trapping

Trapping is the most universally applicable and dependable way to control moles. Mole traps are available at hardware stores, nurseries, or directly from online or catalog outlets. Keep in mind that the best mole traps differ from those for pocket gophers; very few traps are effective for both animals.

Understanding mole behavior helps improve trapping. To be effective, the trap must be set to catch the mole underground. When a mole's sensitive snout encounters something strange in the burrow, it is likely to plug off that portion and dig around or under the object. Traps should generally be set to straddle or encircle the tunnel or be suspended above it. Most mole traps operate on the theory that a mole will push its way through a soil block in its tunnel because cave-ins happen naturally. The upward pressure of the mole's body or the movement of soil against a triggering plate springs the trap.

Moles are active throughout the year and can be trapped at any time. Before setting mole traps, determine which runways are in current use. Moles dig a system of deep tunnels as

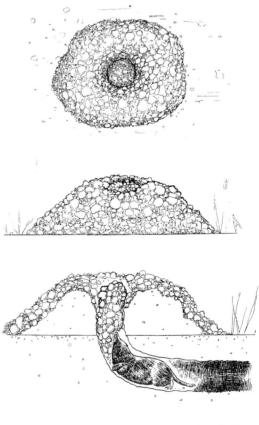

FIGURE 72.

Mounds are formed when moles push soil up out of the burrow.

FIGURE 73.

Moles create surface burrows when searching for insects.

of activity. Select a frequently used runway to increase the success of your control efforts. Set traps at least 18 inches (0.5 m) from a mound in runways frequently used by the mole. Locate deeper tunnels by probing between mounds or next to a fresh mound with a pointed stick, slender metal rod, or gopher probe (see the chapter on pocket gophers for more information). When the earth suddenly gives way, the probe has probably broken through to the burrow.

Mole traps are fairly expensive, so most people tend to buy only one. Although one trap may solve the problem, increasing the number of traps increases the speed and overall success of the trapping program. In California, two types of mole traps are most commonly used: the scissor-jaw type and the harpoon type. Moles have sometimes been caught with pincer-type gopher traps set in mole runways, but these are rarely as effective as the scissor-jaw or harpoon traps. Trap manufacturers often provide detailed instructions that should be followed carefully.

Set the scissor-jaw trap in the mole's main underground tunnel, usually 8 to 12 inches (20.5 to 30.5 cm) deep (figs. 74–75). Using a garden trowel or small shovel, remove a section of

well as a network of surface runs for feeding. Most of the surface tunnels are temporary and may not be good places to set traps because they may not be reused. Deep runways are more or less permanently used.

To determine where moles are active, tamp down short sections of surface runways and mounds. Observe these areas daily and re-tamp any raised sections, making note of the areas

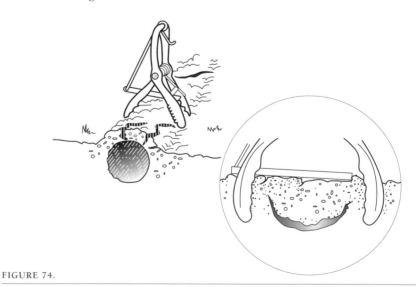

FIGURE 74.

Scissor-jaw mole trap straddling a surface tunnel. The insert shows how the trigger pan rests on the depressed ridge when set.

FIGURE 75.

Scissor-jaw trap installed in a main tunnel.

FIGURE 76.

Harpoon trap installed in a mole tunnel.

FIGURE 77.

Despite claims made by manufacturers, vibrating and noise-making windmills have little repellent effect on moles.

soil slightly larger than the trap width, about 6 inches (15 cm). Build a plug of soil in the center of the opened runway for the trigger pan to rest on. Moist soil from the opened tunnel or from a nearby fresh mound can be squeezed together to build the plug. Wedge the set trap, with safety catch in place, firmly into the opened burrow with the trigger placed snugly against the top of the soil plug. Scatter loose soil onto the set trap to about the level of the top of the tunnel. This excludes light from the opened burrow and probably makes the mole less suspicious of the plugged tunnel. Release the safety catch.

Harpoon traps (fig. 76) work in the deeper tunnels if you set them on a soil plug as described for the scissor-jaw trap. They can also be set on the surface over an active runway ridge that has been pressed down under the trigger pan. To install a harpoon trap, depress a small portion of the ridge about halfway down to the bottom of the tunnel and set the trap so that the trigger rests lightly on the depressed area. The trap will be set off when the mole attempts to pass through the depressed section of the tunnel. Place a plastic pail over the trap to prevent pets or other animals from disturbing the trap.

Repellents

Several repellents have been suggested for controlling moles. Home remedies include placing irritating materials such as broken glass, razor blades, thorny rose bush branches, bleach, mothballs, lye, castor oil, and even human hair in the burrow in an effort to drive moles away. Frightening devices such as mole-wheels, vibrating windmills, and whistling bottles are also commonly referred to in garden literature (fig. 77). Various electrical soil-vibrating or sound-producing devices are also advertised for mole control. Some garden literature notes that the gopher or mole plant (*Euphorbia lathyris*) can be used as a repellent. None of these repellent-based methods has proved to be successful in stopping mole damage or in driving moles from an area, and commercially available mole repellents have little data to prove that they are effective.

Toxic Baits

Because the mole's main diet is earthworms and insects, poisoning them with dry-grain-based baits is rarely effective. Recently, however, two new innovative bait products have been introduced, a gel-type warfarin bait and a bromethalin-laden artificial worm. Little independent field research has been conducted on the effectiveness of these promising products.

Other Control Methods

Some gardeners have found that moles can be detected by watching for "moving" ridges caused when a mole digs surface runs. If you can see such movements, try using a shovel or other garden tool to dislodge and dispatch the animal.

Underground fencing as described for pocket gophers may provide temporary control of moles, but because of their burrowing abilities the control does not last long. Wire mesh baskets prevent planted bulbs from being heaved out of the ground, and wire mesh bottoms used in raised beds totally exclude moles.

Flooding moles out of an area with water or fumigating them with smoke or gas cartridges have had little success, but they may be worth trying if the effort is persistent. In theory, if moles are deprived of their food supply, they should move to other areas to find food. Insecticide treatments to control soil insect pests may decrease the food available for moles. These insect control programs must be conducted according to label instructions. This method may not be effective to control moles and, if effective, is likely to be a very slow process.

MONITORING GUIDELINES

Once you have controlled damage, establish a system to monitor for reinfestation. Mounds and surface runways are obvious indicators of the presence of moles. Because mole damage can be unsightly, make lawn maintenance difficult, and destroy valuable plants, the number of moles that can be tolerated is usually quite low, sometimes even zero. As soon as you see an active mound or surface runway, begin trapping, which is the most effective and appropriate control action.

OPOSSUMS

The opossum (*Didelphis virginiana*), family Didelphidae, is the only native North American marsupial (animals that carry their young in an abdominal pouch). It is not, however, native to California; it was introduced many years ago and has now become well established throughout much of the state. Opossums are about the size of a house cat and have coarse grayish fur, a pointed face, and hairless rounded ears (fig. 78). They are about 2 to 3 feet (0.6 to 0.9 m) long, including the hairless tail, and weigh up to 15 pounds (6.8 kg). Males are usually larger than females. Their feet resemble small hands with widely spread fingers. Opossums are well adapted for climbing. Their long, hairless, prehensile tail and opposable toe on the hind foot assist in holding on to small branches or similar structures. Opossums can also carry nesting materials and other items with their tails.

FIGURE 78.

Opossum.

Their natural habitats are diverse, ranging from arid to moist and from wooded to open fields, but they prefer environments near streams or wetlands. They take shelter in abandoned burrows of other animals, tree cavities, brush piles, and beneath other dense cover. In urban and suburban settings they may den under steps, porches, decks, garden sheds, and if accessible, in attics, garages, and beneath houses, where they make an untidy nest. The old belief that opossums are nomadic without well-developed home ranges has been disproved. They have complex but flexible social relationships with overlapping home ranges that allow high populations to develop when food is plentiful.

In its nocturnal foraging the opossum is a true omnivore, feeding on fruits, nuts, green plants, insects, snakes, frogs, birds and their eggs, and small mammals such as meadow voles (fig. 79). It eats both fresh meat and carrion and is often seen feeding on road kills, a habit that makes it vulnerable to being struck by a passing car and killed. Opossums that live near people may visit vegetable gardens, compost piles, garbage cans, or food dishes intended for dogs or cats. Having lost much of their natural fear of people, they will enter a home through a pet door in a search for food. Fortunately, they are not aggressive unless cornered.

Their mating season extends from January to July; two litters are produced averaging about 7 young each (fig. 80). After a short 13-day gestation period, the ½-inch-long (12.5-mm) young are born. Like other marsupials, the blind, helpless young find their way into the mother's pouch, where each attaches to one of the 13 teats. They do not let go for about 8 weeks, during which they continue their development and growth. At approximately 11 weeks of age they can leave the pouch for short periods. When the young become too large for all to fit inside the pouch at one time, some will ride along by hanging on to the mother's back. The young are weaned at about 14 weeks. Females mate again after the first litter of the season is able to live alone. The second litter will be sufficiently grown to leave the mother by fall. Mortality in the young is high; most perish before they are a year old. Young that survive until the next spring will breed. Few opossums live beyond 3 years.

FIGURE 79.

Opossums are omnivorous and feed on a wide variety of items. They are especially fond of eggs.

Opossums have a maximum running speed of only 7 miles per hour (11.3 km/h), so they have developed strategies to escape enemies. They readily enter burrows and climb trees in an attempt to elude danger. When threatened, an opossum may bare its teeth, growl, hiss, and exude a repulsive smelly musklike fluid from its anal glands, which offers some degree of protection from predators. "Playing possum" is another characteristic

FIGURE 80.

Opossum in nest with young.

reaction: the animal rolls over on its side, becomes limp, shuts its eyes, and lets its tongue hang from an open mouth. The heartbeat slows and the animal appears to be dead. This reaction is a nervous shock from which the opossum recovers quickly and is able to take the first opportunity to escape. When surprised during daylight, opossums appear bewildered and sluggish.

Opossums are considered a nuisance in gardens and near homes where they feed on berries, grapes, and tree fruits and nuts, and defecate on garden paths and patios. They fight with dogs and cats and can inflict serious injury with their sharp, pointed teeth.

Opossums carry diseases such as leptospirosis, tuberculosis, relapsing fever, tularemia, spotted fever, toxoplasmosis, coccidiosis, trichomoniasis, and Chagas' disease. They may also be infested with fleas, ticks, mites, and lice. Opossums are hosts for cat and dog fleas, especially in urban environments.

LEGAL RESTRAINTS OF CONTROL

The California Fish and Game Code classifies opossums as nongame mammals. If you find opossums threatening growing crops or other property of which you are the owner or tenant, you may control them using any legal means. Department of Fish and Game regulations prohibit the relocation of wildlife without written permission from the DFG. Check to make sure that there are no local restrictions pertaining to the removal of opossums prior to taking any action.

CONTROL METHODS

The control methods for opossums are the same or similar to those for skunks and raccoons. Opossums generally do not become as numerous as raccoons can and are not as objectionable as skunks. Opossums are highly adaptable and are great survivors. Once they have invaded a neighborhood they are probably there to stay as long as food, water, and shelter are available.

Habitat Control

The aim of habitat control is to make your premises less appealing to the opossum. Cut back overgrown shrubbery and trim trees that overhang rooftops at least 5 feet (1.5 m) from the roof edge. Pick up and dispose of fallen fruit. Stack your firewood tightly, leaving no gaps suitable for a den. Store scrap lumber and other items in an orderly manner, preferably about 18 inches (0.5 m) off the ground. Garbage cans should have tight-fitting lids. Do not place food items or table scraps in your compost pile or bin. Food placed outdoors for pets should be removed by nightfall.

Exclusion

As with skunks and raccoons, the best solution to opossum problems beneath stairs, porches, decks, or buildings is to screen or block them out. Close off all potential entrances or openings under the house, garden shed, mobile home, deck, and so on with ¼-inch (6.5-mm) mesh hardware cloth. This small mesh also excludes rats and house mice.

Once an opossum has taken up residence beneath a building or deck make sure the animal has left before blocking the opening. A fairly easy way to determine this is to sprinkle a smooth layer of flour about ⅛ inch (3 mm) thick in front of the entrance to form a tracking patch in which the animal's footprints will be evident. Examine the tracking patch soon after dark; the presence of footprints indicates that the animal has left and the opening can be closed off. Opossums usually live alone except when with young, and the young leave the den with the mother.

Opossums can also be excluded from gardens by a fence built of poultry wire. The fence should be 4 feet (1.2 m) high with the top 12 to 18 inches (0.3 to 0.5 m) of the fence bent outward, away from the garden, and not attached to any support. Since the top of the fence is not rigid and bends under the animal's weight, the animal cannot climb over it. As an alternative, any standard wire fence can be made

What to Do If Bitten by a Wild Animal

If you are bitten or scratched by a wild animal, clean the wound by thoroughly scrubbing it with soap and water as soon as possible to reduce the chance of infection. If soap is not available, wash thoroughly with clean water.

All wounds inflicted by wild animals should be examined by a physician, who will determine the course of treatment, if any, based on the offending species and the seriousness of the wound. Quick medical attention reduces the incidence of infection and disease. Puncture-type wounds are considered to be especially serious, even if they do not appear to be so.

Animals known to be vectors of rabies should always be regarded as rabid, and their bite should be treated accordingly. Bats and skunks top that list in California.

opossum-proof by stretching an electrically charged wire in front of the top of the fence 3 inches (7.5 cm) out from the mesh. Use a cattle-type electric fence charger to activate the wire. A similar approach can prevent opossums from climbing trees. For more information on electric fencing, see the chapter on raccoons.

Trapping

Opossums are not wary of traps and can easily be caught with a box- or cage-type live-catch trap. Traps should be at least 10 by 12 by 32 inches (25.5 by 30.5 by 81 cm) in size and should be set along trails or known routes of travel. Fish-flavored canned cat food works well as trap bait, but it often attracts cats as well. To avoid this possibility, try using whole raw chicken eggs or jam or peanut butter spread on a bit of bread. Other baits can include overripe fruit such as grapes, bananas, or melon. Live trapping presents the problem of dealing with the animal once captured. Since it is illegal to relocate an opossum without a permit, those not wanting to deal with its disposal may prefer to hire a professional wildlife control operator. They are equipped to handle problem wildlife in a legal and humane manner. You can find them listed under the pest control, animal control, or wildlife control headings in the yellow pages of the telephone book.

Other Control Methods

A motion-activated sprinkler device sometimes induces a fright response in opossums, skunks, and raccoons. If the animal has established the habit of visiting the yard or garden, this frightening rarely lasts for more than a few days. A greater effect is observed on animals that have not habituated to the site.

An array of chemical products is marketed for repelling various wildlife species, but, unfortunately, none offer significant results. The odor of mothballs or naphthalene crystals, used as a home remedy repellent, has occasionally been reported to be successful in driving opossums from confined areas.

No toxicants are registered for poisoning opossums. Poison baits sold for the control of rodents should never be used in an attempt to control opossums, skunks, or raccoons. The penalty for such pesticide misuse can be substantial, and the practice usually comes to light as a result of the accidental poisoning of someone's pet.

In rural areas where it is legal and safe to do so, opossums may be spotlighted at night and shot.

MONITORING GUIDELINES

Because they are active at night, opossums may never be seen as they travel through neighborhoods or yards. Barking dogs and disappearing pet food left out overnight may be the first apparent clues. Strange-looking droppings may be found on garden paths, walkways, and patios. Since opossums are messy feeders, you may find remnants of the previous night's foraging and feeding. An occasional visit by an opossum or a family of opossums may not present cause for concern unless you have pets that remain outdoors at night. Pet and opossum confrontations are relatively common, and the pets are often injured. Early action may be warranted to avoid such a problem.

POCKET GOPHERS

Pocket gophers (*Thomomys* spp.) are stout-bodied, short-legged rodents in the family Geomyidae that are well adapted for burrowing. In California, the Botta's pocket gopher *(T. bottae)* is the most common species (fig. 81). Pocket gophers live alone in an extensive underground burrow system that can cover an area of several hundred square feet (fig. 82). These burrows are about 2 to 3 inches (5 to 7.5 cm) in diameter and are usually located from 6 to 14 inches (15 to 35.5 cm) below ground. Pocket gophers often invade gardens and lawns, where they feed mostly underground on a wide variety of roots, bulbs, tubers, grasses, and seeds, and sometimes even the bark at the base of trees (fig. 83). Their feeding and burrowing can damage lawns, ornamental plants, vegetables, forbs, vines, and trees (fig. 84). In addition, their gnawing may damage plastic water lines, lawn sprinkler systems, and buried utility and communication lines. Their tunnels can divert and carry off irrigation water, lead to excessive soil erosion, and may cause some structures to fall.

Pocket gophers range in length from 6 to 12 inches (15 to 30.5 cm). They have a thick body with little evidence of a neck, and their eyes and ears are quite small; their front claws are curved. Their common name is derived from their fur-lined external cheek pouches, or pockets, in which they carry food and nesting materials. The pocket gopher's lips close behind its four large incisor teeth, keeping dirt out of its mouth when it uses its teeth for digging.

Pocket gophers rarely travel above ground except for when the young are dispersing to new sites. They are sometimes seen while feeding, pushing dirt out of their burrow system. The mounds of fresh soil that are the result of burrow

FIGURE 81.

Botta's pocket gopher.

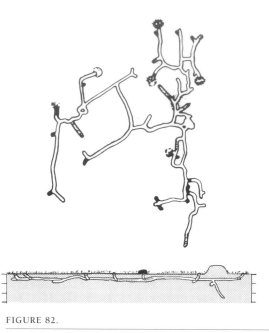

FIGURE 82.

Aerial view and cross-section of typical pocket gopher burrow.

excavation indicate their presence (fig. 85). Their mounds are usually crescent shaped and are located at the ends of short lateral tunnels branching from a main burrow system. One gopher may push up several mounds in a day. They are active day and night, year round. The lack of fresh mounding is not an indication that they are not present and active, since gophers at times fail to produce mounds and in turn backfill old tunnels with the excavated soil.

LEGAL RESTRAINTS OF CONTROL

The California Fish and Game Code classifies pocket gophers as nongame mammals. If you find pocket gophers threatening growing crops or other property of which you are the owner or tenant, you may control the gophers using any legal means.

CONTROL METHODS

Because of the nature of pocket gopher damage, a successful control program depends on early detection and prompt action. Most people control gophers in lawns, gardens, or small orchards by trapping or using poison baits placed by hand. A program incorporating these methods should

FIGURE 83.

Pocket gopher girdling of a pine tree.

FIGURE 84.

Pocket gopher girdling has caused this grape vine to die back.

FIGURE 85.

Typical crescent-shaped pocket gopher mound.

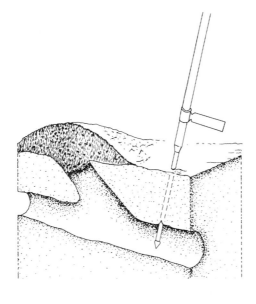

FIGURE 86.

A gopher probe drops suddenly when it enters a tunnel. Probes can also be used to find mole tunnels by probing in a circle around a fresh molehill.

result in significant reduction in pocket gopher damage.

Successful trapping or baiting depends on accurately locating the gopher's active main tunnel or burrow, which is usually 6 to 14 inches (15 to 35.5 cm) deep. The crescent-shaped mounds visible above ground are connected to this burrow by short lateral tunnels. Because gophers plug the lateral tunnels, trapping and baiting in them is not as successful as in the main tunnel system.

To locate the main burrow, use a gopher probe. Gopher probes are commercially available or can be constructed from a pipe, wooden dowel, or stick; some are equipped to dispense toxic bait (fig. 86). Look for the freshest mounds because they indicate an area of recent gopher activity. You will usually see a small circle or depression representing the plugged lateral tunnel. This plug is generally bordered on three sides by soil, making the mound crescent-shaped. Begin probing 8 to 12 inches (20.5 to 30.5 cm) from the plugged side of the mound. When the probe penetrates the gopher's burrow, it should suddenly drop about 2 inches (5 cm). Often, the main burrow runs between two mounds. To locate the main burrow you may have to probe repeatedly, but your skill in locating the tunnel will improve with experience.

Trapping

Trapping can be a safe and effective method to control pocket gophers. Several types of gopher traps are available. Two common traps are the two-pronged pincer trap and the squeeze-type box trap (fig. 87). These traps are triggered when the gopher pushes against a flat vertical pan or wire trigger.

After you have located the main tunnel, open it with a shovel or garden trowel and set traps in pairs

FIGURE 87.

Three box-type gopher traps.

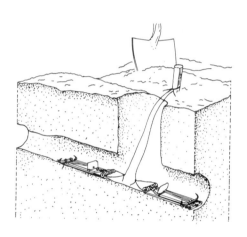

FIGURE 88.

Placement of box-type traps in gopher hole.

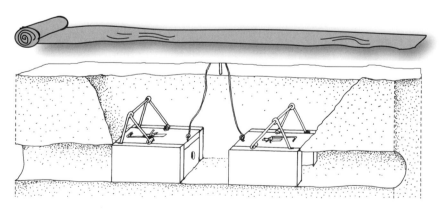

FIGURE 89.

After placing box-type traps for gopher control, fill in the openings so that no light enters the hole.

facing opposite directions (fig. 88). This placement intercepts a gopher coming from either end of the burrow. The box trap is generally easier to set but requires more excavation, an important consideration in lawns and some gardens. Box traps are especially useful when the gopher's main burrow is less than 3 inches (7.5 cm) in diameter, because small burrows must be enlarged to accommodate wire pincer traps. All traps should be wired to stakes to make them easier to keep track of. After setting the traps, exclude light from the burrow by covering the opening with dirt clods, sod, cardboard, or some other material (fig. 89). Fine soil can be sifted around the edges to ensure a light-tight seal. If light enters, the gopher may plug the burrow with soil, filling the traps and making them ineffective. Check traps often and reset them when necessary. If no gopher is caught within 2 to 3 days, reset the traps in a different location. Human odor on traps has no apparent effect on trapping success.

Toxic Baits

Strychnine-treated bait is the best and most common rodenticide used for pocket gopher control. These baits are effective with one application. Zinc phosphide gopher baits are also available but they are not as effective for the species of pocket gophers found in California. Paraffin bait bars containing an anticoagulant are generally available for pocket gopher control. The loose-grain anticoagulant bait may be more difficult to find, but it may be available from your local county agricultural commissioner. All gopher bait is poisonous and should be used and stored with caution. Because gopher bait is placed underground, it is considered relatively safe to use since it is not exposed to most other animals or to children. However, animals such as dogs can dig up gophers and might be exposed to bait in this way. Read and follow product label instructions carefully.

Always place pocket gopher baits in the gopher's underground tunnel. After locating the main burrow with a probe, enlarge the opening by rotating the probe or inserting a larger rod or stick. Place the bait carefully in the opening, taking care not to spill any on the ground surface. A funnel can help prevent spillage (fig. 90). Close the probe hole with sod, rock, paper, or some other material to exclude light and prevent dirt from falling on the bait.

An alternative method is to apply the strychnine bait through a reservoir-type gopher probe (fig. 91). This device has a built-in holding compartment for the bait and a long hollow shank with a trigger and measuring mechanism. Probe with the device into the gopher's tunnel, then activate it to meter a prescribed amount of bait into the burrow (fig. 92). These probes, which

FIGURE 90.

Use a funnel when spooning strychnine bait into a gopher tunnel through a probe hole.

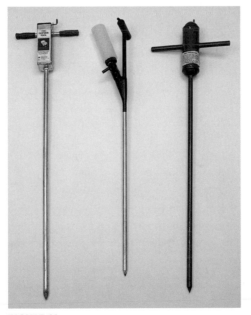

FIGURE 91.

Reservoir-type gopher probes for dispensing bait. Using these probes greatly speeds baiting.

FIGURE 92.

Dispensing bait using a reservoir-type gopher probe.

FIGURE 93.

Lining the bottom of a raised bed with wire mesh excludes gophers as well as moles.

FIGURE 94.

Planting baskets made of 1-inch chicken wire protect bulbs from pocket gophers. Leave about 3 inches (7.5 cm) of the basket exposed above the ground.

are available commercially, greatly speed up the control procedure, especially when a significant population exists. They are designed for applying acute toxicants such as strychnine and zinc phosphide baits, but they are not suitable for use with anticoagulants baits that require substantially larger quantities of bait per placement.

To measure your success, tamp down or rake existing mounds so that you can distinguish new activity from the old. If gopher-mounding activity continues for more than 2 days after strychnine application, or 10 to 15 days after anticoagulant baits have been used, repeat your baiting efforts.

Exclusion

Temporary protection from gophers may be achieved by using a 3-foot (1-m) or wider roll of ½-inch (12.5-mm) wire mesh buried at a depth of 2 feet (0.6 m), with a 6-inch (15-cm) flare turned away from the area to be protected. Unfortunately, this labor-intensive belowground fence will over time be breached by the gophers' extensive burrowing activity. Small areas such as bulb beds may be protected from pocket gophers by complete underground screening with ½-inch wire mesh. If wire is used, be careful to place it deep enough so that it will not restrict root growth. Raised beds offer excellent protection from gophers and moles when the bottom of the bed is lined with wire mesh (fig. 93). Wire mesh baskets can be purchased or made in which to plant bulbs (fig. 94). Larger wire baskets can be made to accommodate fruit trees, but the basket can interfere with root growth. One way to install the basket is to line the planning hole with wire mesh. The common recommendation is a hole as deep as the root ball and twice its diameter. For bare-root planting, the hole should be large enough so the roots can be planted without restriction. For the best protection, at least 6 inches (15 cm) of the wire basket should project above ground level.

Other Control Methods

Although pocket gophers can easily withstand normal garden or landscape irrigation, flooding can sometimes force them out of their burrows, making them vulnerable and easier to capture. This procedure is most likely to be effective if your garden has been just recently invaded. Fumigation with smoke or gas cartridges is usually not effective because gophers quickly seal off their burrow when they detect smoke or gas. Do not to use fumigants near or under buildings since this can be very hazardous to building inhabitants. Read and follow the label instructions carefully.

Repellents are not effective in protecting gardens or other plantings from pocket gophers. The plant gopher spurge (*Euphorbia lathyris*) has been suggested as a repellent, but no scientific evidence supports its effectiveness. Frightening gophers with sounds, vibrations, electromagnetic devices, or other means has not been effective in driving them from an area or preventing their damage.

In areas where severe gopher problems persist, you may want to contact a professional pest control operator. They are experienced in gopher control and have access to other methods, such as aluminum phosphide fumigation, that are not available to the public.

Biological Control

As is the case with other small rodents, a number of predators, such as hawks, owls, fox, coyotes, and snakes, feed on pocket gophers (fig. 95). The fact that gophers do not spend much time above ground limits their vulnerability. Some gardeners welcome predators such as barn owls and provide nest boxes to encourage their presence. The problem is that all the possible predators combined cannot eliminate a gopher population, and even one or two gophers can devastate a garden.

Dogs and cats that are good hunters may offer some assistance in killing invading gophers before they become well established. In the process, however, dogs may dig up and destroy your lawn or garden. Once gophers become well established, the effectiveness of pets is much reduced.

FIGURE 95.

Gopher snake in the process of devouring a pocket gopher. Because this snake may not eat again for several months, snakes have little impact on pocket gopher numbers.

MONITORING GUIDELINES

Once pocket gopher damage has been controlled, establish a system to monitor the area for reinfestation. Level or tamp down all existing mounds after the control program and clean away weeds and garden debris so fresh mounds can be easily detected. A monitoring program is important because pocket gophers may move in from other areas and cause more damage in a short time, probably by using the tunnels left by the previous occupants. Experience has shown that it is easier, less expensive, and less time-consuming to control gophers before their numbers build up to where they cause excessive damage.

Rabbits

Rabbits are enjoyed by many people, but they can be very destructive in gardens and landscaped areas. They eat a wide variety of plants, including grasses, grains, alfalfa, vegetables, fruit trees, vines, and many ornamentals (figs. 96–99). Rabbits can also damage plastic irrigation systems by gnawing on them. Although there is some variation in the way the terms are used, "rabbit" generally refers to the smaller, brush-dwelling animals with relatively short ears and legs, such as the cottontail, and "hare" generally refers to the larger animals that have longer legs and ears and inhabit more-open areas, such as the jackrabbit. In this publication, "rabbit" applies to both types.

Three rabbits (family Leporidae) are common in California: the black-tailed jackrabbit (*Lepus californicus*), the cottontail (*Sylvilagus audubonii*), and the brush rabbit (*S. bachmani*). Because of its greater size and abundance, the jackrabbit is the most destructive of the three in California, especially in agricultural areas. Cottontails are common pests in landscaped areas, particularly in Southern California. Brush rabbits are similar to cottontails and are somewhat less frequently seen.

The jackrabbit is about the size of a house cat, 17 to 22 inches (43 to 56 cm) long. It has long ears, short front legs, and long hind legs (fig. 100). Jackrabbits typically occupy open or semiopen lands in California valleys and foothills (fig. 101). They do not build a nest but make a depression in the soil beneath a bush or other vegetation. When born, young jackrabbits are fully haired and their eyes

FIGURE 96.

Cottontails live in these juniper shrubs and feed on the turf at dusk.

are open. Within a few days, they can move about quite rapidly. The breeding season varies from February through May or longer and produces from 2 to 6 litters per year with litter sizes of 2 to 4.

Cottontail and brush rabbits are smaller and have shorter ears (fig. 102). They inhabit brushy areas where the cover is dense. Landscaped areas can provide excellent habitat. They are often found beneath junipers and other large, low-growing evergreen shrubs. They can also find cover under piles of rocks or debris.

LEGAL RESTRAINTS OF CONTROL

The California Fish and Game Code classifies jackrabbits as game mammals. If they injure growing crops or other property, they may be taken (killed) at any time by the owner or tenant of the premises. Cottontails and brush rabbits are also game mammals, and may be taken by the owner or tenant of the land, or by any person authorized in writing by such owner or tenant, when the rabbits are damaging crops or forage. Local interpretations of Fish and Game regulations exist, so check with the local DFG if rabbits are causing problems in landscaped areas. Any person other than the owner or tenant of the land must carry written authority from the owner or tenant of the land where the rabbits were taken when rabbits are transported from the

FIGURE 97.

Ornamental grass clumps severely damaged by jackrabbits.

FIGURE 98.

This stem has been clipped by a jackrabbit at the characteristic 45° angle.

FIGURE 99.

Jackrabbit damage to the trunk of a young peach tree.

property. Rabbits taken in these ways cannot be sold for fur or meat. Since laws and regulations change frequently, check with the local DFG warden about the current status of rabbit control, especially in landscaped areas.

FIGURE 100.

Black-tailed jackrabbit.

FIGURE 101.

Jackrabbits can often be seen loafing in open areas during daylight hours.

CONTROL METHODS

A number of methods can reduce rabbit damage, but physical exclusion, trapping, and, to a lesser degree, repellents are recommended for protecting gardens and landscaped areas. In cases where these methods are not practical, contact your local University of California Cooperative Extension farm advisor or county agricultural commissioner for further information.

Exclusion

Fences, if properly built, can be very effective in keeping rabbits out of an area. A fence 30 to 36 inches (0.8 to 0.9 m) tall made of 1-inch (2.5-cm) or smaller mesh, with the bottom turned outward and buried 6 inches (15 cm) deep, will exclude rabbits. Include tight-fitting gates with sills to keep rabbits from digging below the bottom rails. Keep gates closed as much as possible because rabbits can be active during the day or at night. Inspect the fence regularly to make sure rabbits or other animals have not dug under it. Poultry netting supported by stakes is adequate for rabbit control, but larger animals, especially livestock, can damage it easily. Cottontail and brush rabbits will not jump a 2-foot (0.6-m)

FIGURE 102.

Cottontail rabbit in front of its burrow.

fence; jackrabbits will jump one only if they are being chased by dogs or are otherwise frightened. Discourage jumping by increasing the aboveground height to 3 feet (0.9 m). Several strands of wire strung above the wire mesh may also increase the height of the fence. If a rabbit gets into the fenced area, you may have to open up a corner to let the rabbit escape. Deer or other fencing may be adapted to exclude rabbits by adding fine wire mesh at the base and burying the mesh 6 inches (15 cm) underground (fig. 103). Temporary fencing made of chicken wire and removable stakes may be the best solution for small garden areas (fig. 104).

In many places, protecting individual plants may be more practical than attempting to exclude rabbits from the entire garden (fig. 105). Plastic tubes or other commercial protectors placed around the trunks of young trees and shrubs can be very effective (fig. 106). You can make trunk protectors by forming 1-inch (2.5-cm) mesh poultry netting that is 18 to 24 inches (0.5 to 0.6 m) wide into cylinders; bury the bottom 2 to 3 inches (5 to 7.5 cm) and brace the cylinder away from the trunk so rabbits cannot press against the trees or foliage and nibble through the mesh. As you would with a protective fence, inspect these barriers regularly.

Repellents

Several chemical repellents are registered for controlling rabbits, and some of them can reduce or prevent rabbit damage to trees, vines, or ornamentals. Rabbits may be repelled by the unpleasant taste of treated plants and move on to other more palatable choices. If plants or crops are for consumption by people, the repellent must be registered for such use. If rabbits are hungry, or if the garden contains highly preferred foods, repellents will probably not be very effective. Most repellents should be applied before or immediately following the first damage and must be reapplied frequently, especially after a rain, heavy dew, sprinkler irrigation, or when new growth occurs. Always follow the label directions for the repellent you are using. Even if the repellents are effective at first, rabbits usually become accustomed to them and their effectiveness quickly diminishes. Repellent formulations

FIGURE 103.

A 7-foot deer fence can be made rabbit-proof and even meadow vole–proof by adding ½-inch wire mesh at the base and burying the mesh underground. Rabbit fences must be buried securely in the ground to prevent rabbits from digging underneath them.

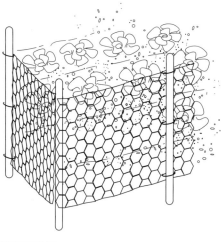

FIGURE 104.

Temporary fencing can exclude rabbits during the growing season.

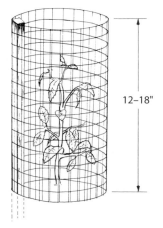

12–18"

FIGURE 105.

Individual plant protectors can be made from 1-inch mesh wire. Bury the wire 2 to 3 inches (5 to 7.5 cm) below the surface.

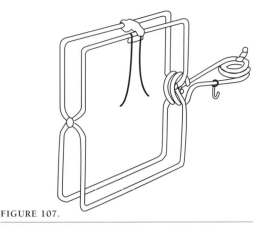

FIGURE 107.

Conibear trap in set position. Place bait behind the trap.

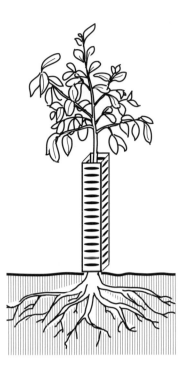

FIGURE 106.

Cardboard or plastic tree guards protect the trunks of young trees from rabbit damage.

based on predator odors, such as urine, may work for a short time (less than 1 week). Rabbits quickly become conditioned to the smell of these natural odors when there is no associated threat.

Trapping

Cottontail and brush rabbits are relatively easy to trap alive; however, jackrabbits are very difficult to capture in this manner because of their reluctance to enter a confining space. Disposal of live rabbits is an additional concern. Since they can carry diseases such as tularemia and are considered agricultural pests, the Fish and Game Code prohibits relocation and release. Captured live rabbits can be dispatched by quickly breaking their necks, although experience is necessary. Euthanasia with carbon dioxide (CO_2) gas is also allowed. If you are confronted with a serious rabbit problem, you may want to hire a wildlife pest control operator to resolve the problem for you.

A few kinds of kill traps are effective for cottontails and brush rabbits. For example, the Conibear 110 or 120 trap placed in a trap box is effective (figs. 107–108). Other rabbit kill traps are available but may have to be ordered from a trap supply firm. These traps should be baited but not set and placed in gardens where rabbits are feeding or have been seen. Rolled barley, apples, carrots, cabbage, lettuce, or whatever rabbits are feeding on in your garden can be used as bait. After the rabbits have been taking the bait for a couple of days, rebait and set the traps. Three to six traps may be needed for a garden; just one will rarely be enough. Be aware that traps may present a potential hazard to nontarget species, so use caution and good judgment when setting kill traps.

Other Control Methods

Shooting can control rabbits, with best results achieved in early morning or in the evening when rabbits are most active. Check local regulations for any restrictions on shooting in your area. Dogs and cats are capable of killing

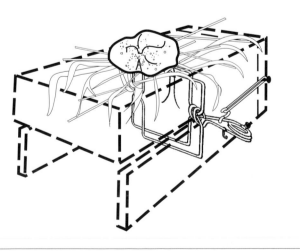

FIGURE 108.

Camouflage the trap box to blend in with rabbit habitat. A trap box that contains a Conibear 110 or 120 trap can capture rabbits, skunks, or ground squirrels. The long length of the box provides some protection for nontarget animals.

rabbits, especially young rabbits, and may assist in keeping the population down. Predators such as hawks and coyotes also eat rabbits. However, in most cases, predators are unable to keep rabbit populations below damaging levels.

MONITORING GUIDELINES

Rabbits are mostly nocturnal, but they are sometimes seen during the daylight hours in areas where they may simply be "loafing." Rabbit sign, such as feeding damage, trails, and droppings, indicates their presence. Because few, if any, rabbits can be tolerated in a garden or landscaped area, take appropriate action when the first sign of rabbits is observed. Rabbits that have been seen nearby frequently invade gardens when the plantings become desirable to them. Therefore, consider exclusion methods or some other control program before serious damage occurs. For jackrabbits, an areawide control program may offer the best results, but such a program can be difficult to organize.

Raccoons

The raccoon (*Procyon lotor*) is a stocky mammal about 2 to 3 feet (0.6 to 0.9 m) long and weighing 10 to 30 pounds (4.5 to 13.6 kg). It is distinctively marked with a black "mask" over the eyes and is heavily furred, with alternating light and dark rings around its tail (fig. 109). Raccoons are active year-round but may hole up in dens during periods of severe winter weather.

Raccoons prefer wooded areas near water and in natural habitats, where they den in hollow trees, ground burrows, brush piles, or rock crevices. However, this nocturnal animal adapts extremely well to urban and suburban environments, where they often den in backyards, beneath decks, or in accessible outbuildings. Attics, chimneys, and the space beneath houses are also used as dens if they can gain access. Because of their nighttime activity, they are often present but may go undetected for some time.

Raccoons are omnivorous, eating plants and animals. Plant foods include fruits, berries, nuts, acorns, corn, and other types of grain. Animal foods include crayfish, clams, fish, frogs, snails, insects, turtles, rabbits, muskrats, and the eggs and young of ground-nesting birds, including waterfowl. In urban settings, in addition to feeding on backyard fruits, nuts, and vegetables, they scavenge from

FIGURE 109.

Raccoons have a distinctively marked black "mask."

garbage cans and compost piles . Pet food left outside overnight ranks high as a food resource. Some people deliberately provide food for raccoons.

Young are generally born in April or May, but earlier and later litters are not uncommon. Litter size ranges from 3 to 6 young, averaging about 4. Family groups usually remain together for the first year, and the year-old young begin to assert their independence the following year when the new litter arrives (fig. 110). Because of the availability of food and den sites, urban and suburban raccoon populations can become very large.

FIGURE 110.

Half-grown young raccoon scurrying back to its den.

LEGAL RESTRAINTS OF CONTROL

In California raccoons are classified as furbearers. The fur harvest season is set by the DFG, which also determines when and how they may be taken. Raccoons causing damage may be taken at any time by legal means. DFG regulations prohibit the relocation of raccoons and other wildlife without written permission of the DFG. For further information, contact the DFG.

The damage to your garden may be relatively minor compared to the potential damage a raccoon can do to your house. Females in search of nesting sites may rip off shingles, fascia boards, or rooftop ventilators to get into the attic (fig. 111). Once inside the attic, they may tear up and displace ceiling insulation and rip or destroy insulation on heating and air conditioning ducts. They may urinate and defecate in a specific spot in the attic, staining the ceiling and creating an objectionable odor. Ectoparasites such as fleas may infest the attic and migrate to other parts of the house. Uncapped chimneys are often used as den sites, as are spaces beneath porches and decks. Doors covering crawl spaces are sometimes damaged in an effort to den beneath the house.

Raccoons are known to carry a number of diseases and internal parasites (see table 1). The raccoon roundworm, an infection spread to people by the accidental ingestion or inhalation of roundworm eggs from raccoon feces, has caused increased concern in recent years. Roundworm infection can cause serious disabilities, and young children are thought to be most susceptible.

CONTROL METHODS

In some communities raccoon problems have become so severe that they are beyond the efforts of individual homeowners. In these situations, a community effort may be the only effective solution. City parks, greenbelts, golf courses, and highway and street plantings may serve as habitat for raccoons by providing them with den sites and travel routes. Storm drains and street and road culverts are commonly used as dens. Since these areas are under the control or management of a city or other jurisdiction, it is often imperative that the jurisdiction be involved in finding solutions, including invoking and enforcing a ban on feeding raccoons,

FIGURE 111.

Raccoons can be very destructive when searching for a nest site or attempting to enter closed-off areas.

educating the public on how best to handle an areawide urban raccoon problem, discouraging individuals from trapping and illegally relocating animals, which only exacerbates the problem.

Habitat Modification

Raccoons are attracted to gardens or homes because they offer a food resource and potential den sites. Efforts toward reducing available food can include using metal garbage cans on which the lids can be secured. To prevent raccoons from tipping over garbage cans, place them in a rack or tie them to a secure post. Pet food left outdoors should be removed before nightfall. Pick up fallen fruits and nuts frequently. Never intentionally provide food for raccoons, and discourage your neighbors from this practice as well; it only attracts more raccoons.

If possible, remove woodpiles or other materials under or in which raccoons can den. Reduce cover by thinning out overgrown shrubbery. Cut back trees that overhang rooftops if possible, leaving a gap of at least 5 feet (1.5 m) to reduce raccoon access. Consider removing trellises and arbors attached to homes that may facilitate

access to the roof. While habitat modification is often helpful, it is rarely a total solution.

Exclusion

Exclusion is the key to eliminating den sites. Raccoons are powerful animals and can become vicious when cornered. Their front paws are handlike, with toes that are long and flexible with considerable dexterity. Raccoons are known to unhook simple latches.

Ordinary fences will not exclude raccoons from gardens or yards, since they either dig under or climb over them. The animal readily locates weaknesses in fences and will rip off loose boards or enlarge holes in wire fences for easy access. By exploiting the raccoon's sensitivity to electric shock, an ordinary fence can be made raccoon-proof by adding a single electrified strand of wire 8 inches (20.5 cm) above the ground and about 8 inches out from the base of the fence. A pulsating high-voltage low-amperage fence charger, similar to that used for confining cattle, electrifies the fence. Electrified wire wrapped around the trunk of a tree discourages climbing. A low two-wire electric fence can be very effective for excluding raccoons from sweet corn, melons, and other highly preferred crops. Fasten one wire 6 inches (15 cm) and the other 12 inches (30.5 cm) above the ground on evenly spaced wooden posts. The fence charger needs to be activated only from dusk to dawn. This type of low-amperage electric fence can also be installed around a newly laid sod lawn to prevent raccoons from rolling back the new sod in search of insects or grubs. Remove the fence once the turf has taken root. Similar fences are sometimes used around ponds to protect koi and goldfish from raccoons.

Before installing an electric fence, explore the pros and cons of its use and, if one is used, be sure the electric charger is appropriate for the task. Electrified fences are not appropriate for all situations, must be installed properly, and should always be identified with warning signs.

Prevent raccoon access to chimneys by covering them with a spark arrester that meets the fire code of your area. These caps keep raccoons, tree squirrels, rats, and birds out of the chimney. Be sure they are tightly secured to prevent raccoons from pulling them loose.

Open spaces beneath porches, decks, sheds, and so on should be tightly screened with ¼- or ⅓-inch (6.5- or 8.5-mm) galvanized hardware mesh to exclude raccoons. The bottom edge of the wire should be buried at least 6 inches (15 cm) deep, extended outward for 12 inches (30.5 cm), and back-covered with soil. These measures will exclude skunks, opossums, squirrels, and rats as well.

Frightening

A variety of scaring materials, gadgets, and devices are marketed for frightening raccoons and other wildlife. These include flashing lights, sound-producing devices, and water squirting units, all of which can be activated by motion detectors. In addition, radios, scarecrows, flags, and windmills that spin or flutter in the wind have been used. Unfortunately, none of these are very effective and, at best, may frighten only for a few days, after which raccoons seem to ignore them, having learned that they present no real threat.

Repellents

Of the few commercial chemical repellents available to repel various forms of wildlife, none have been proved to be effective for raccoons. Home remedies such as mothballs, blood meal, and a wide variety of other

FIGURE 112.

Raccoons peel back the rolls of newly laid sod in search of grubs and insects. Trapping them is best handled by a pest control professional. An alternative to trapping is to surround the area with a 2-wire electric fence.

materials have been tried to no avail, as raccoons are quick to adapt.

Trapping

The average homeowner who is unfamiliar with trapping raccoons should hire a professional wildlife control operator to remove raccoons (fig. 112). These operators have the proper equipment to accomplish the task and will be able to tell whether a trapped female is nursing young. This is very important because you do not want to leave young behind to starve. Pest control operators also have the means to euthanize the animals, since releasing them elsewhere is prohibited by law; released animals may return or present a problem to someone else. Releasing an animal is a major factor in the dissemination of the numerous diseases they carry to other animals. Some counties have trapping programs for nuisance animals including raccoons. Contact your local county agricultural commissioner to check whether this service is available.

Although raccoons are fairly easy to trap, a clever and cunning individual can occasionally be quite elusive. A single-door live-cage trap is usually the best type for homeowners, although other types may be used by professionals to capture more-difficult animals. The single-door trap should be of sturdy construction and at least 10 by 12 by 32 inches (25.5 by 30.5 by 81 cm) in size. Larger traps, 15 by 15 by 36 inches (38 by 38 by 91.5 cm), are even better. Canned tuna or fish-flavored canned cat food make excellent baits but may also attract nontarget cats and dogs. To avoid catching cats, try using marshmallows, grapes, prunes, peanut butter, or sweet rolls as bait. Place small pieces of bait along a path leading up to the trap. Cover the rear of the trap with ½-inch (12.5-mm) wire mesh to prevent the raccoon from reaching through the trap from the outside to steal the bait. Traps should be well anchored to the ground or weighted to prevent the animal from tipping the trap over to obtain the bait. Set traps at night and close them in the morning to avoid trapping nontarget animals. Raccoons are intelligent and clever. They are also powerful and can be vicious when trapped or cornered. Have a plan in place to destroy trapped animals before you begin trapping.

Other Control Methods

Dogs may alert you to the presence of raccoons and may frighten some of them away. However, raccoons may attack dogs and can seriously injure or even kill them. Since raccoons are usually active at night, and since hunting them generally requires specially bred and trained dogs, shooting them to solve the problem should be left to a professional.

MONITORING GUIDELINES

You may see raccoons in your garden or yard at night, or you may see them peering into your house through glass doors. Evidence of feeding, tracks, and droppings may provide clues to their visits. Noises created by their running on the roof or rustling in the chimney or attic also let you know of their presence. An occasional visit by a raccoon or a family of raccoons may not present a major concern, but if these visits become commonplace and if they are also climbing on your roof or trying to get under your house, action is probably warranted.

RATS AND HOUSE MICE

Worldwide, rats and house mice are some of the most troublesome and damaging rodents, and the West Coast of the United States is no exception. They transmit parasites and diseases to other animals (including people) (see table 1), consume and contaminate food, and damage structures and property. Rats and house mice live and thrive under a wide variety of climates and conditions. They are found in and around homes, farms, gardens, and in natural habitats. House mice are generally not very troublesome in gardens and landscaped areas, but when they are able to gain access to a building, they will no doubt cause some damage. Norway and roof rats can cause significant damage to garden crops and ornamental plantings.

House mice (*Mus musculus*) are small, agile rodents (fig. 113). They have slender bodies, 5 to 7 inches (12.5 to 18 cm) long, and weigh ½ to 1 ounce (14 to 28 g). House mice have rather large ears for their body size, and their semihairless tail is about as long as the body and head combined. House mice eat a wide variety of foods, although they seem to prefer cereal grains (fig. 114). They do not need to drink water to survive and can obtain all of their required moisture from the food they eat. They have keen senses of taste, hearing, smell, and touch and are excellent climbers. In addition, they can squeeze through openings as small as ¼ inch (6.5 mm). They tend to nest in secluded places such as crates, boxes, sacks, drawers, and between walls, and may occupy any area or level of a building where food is available nearby. Outdoors they may nest in woodpiles and beneath or in any stacked material, as long as it remains dry. Mice tend to move

FIGURE 113.

House mouse.

FIGURE 114.

House mouse damage to cereal boxes.

FIGURE 115.

Norway rat.

FIGURE 116.

Norway rats prefer secluded areas near sources of food and water.

inside buildings in the fall, when the weather turns cooler. They are mostly nocturnal and are capable of breeding year round, especially in the warmer climates or in heated buildings. In a single year a female may have 5 to 10 litters, averaging 5 young per litter. They provide numerous signs of their presence, including sounds, droppings, urine stains, smudges and gnaw marks, footprints, nests, and musky mouse odors.

The Norway rat (*Rattus norvegicus*),

sometimes called the brown rat or sewer rat, is much larger than a house mouse, 14 to 18 inches (30.5 to 45.5 cm) long including the tail and averaging 7 to 10 ounces (196 to 280 g) when mature (fig. 115). Its burrows are found along building foundations and beneath concrete slabs, rubbish, or woodpiles. In and around gardens, its burrows may be found beneath compost piles and along fences or other secluded areas near sources of food and water (fig. 116). Norway rats can enter buildings through any opening larger than ½ inch (12.5 mm). When they invade a building, they usually remain in the basement or on the ground floor. In a heated building, they can breed year round. If they live outdoors, the main breeding period is in spring and summer. Norway rats are mostly active at night and feed on a wide variety of foods. They have keen senses of hearing, taste, and smell and can swim and climb quite well.

Roof rats (*Rattus rattus*), sometimes called black rats, are 12 to 16 inches (18 to 20.5 cm) long including the tail, slightly smaller and more slender than Norway rats (fig. 117). Their naked tail is longer than the combined length of their head and body. This feature can distinguish them from the Norway rat, whose tail is shorter than its head and body combined. Roof rats are agile climbers and usually live and nest in dense shrubs, vines, trees, and dense ground cover such as ivy. In buildings they are most often found in enclosed spaces such as attics and cabinets and between walls. They prefer to nest and travel high in a building and not on the ground floor. At night they come down to feed on the ground floor; if they are nesting in an attic they will go outside to feed. They often travel from property to property on overhead telephone or power lines and enter buildings at roof level, wherever a gap or broken vent screen is found.

Because of their nocturnal habits,

FIGURE 117.

Roof rat.

people may not see Norway or roof rats, but their activity provides numerous signs of their presence. These signs include squeaking and scratching noises, droppings, urine stains, smudges and gnaw marks, footprints and tail marks, nests, and food caches. The sound of rats running and rustling around in the attic at night may be one of the first indicators of their presence. Evidence of their presence outdoors may be damage to fruit or vegetables or signs that they have been feeding on pet food left out at night (figs. 118–119). In California, the roof rat has become a common and serious problem in urban and suburban gardens and landscaped areas, especially in the warmer and coastal regions where heavily landscaped plantings occur. They are more difficult to bring under control than are Norway rats.

LEGAL RESTRAINTS OF CONTROL

The California Fish and Game Code classifies rats and mice as nongame mammals. If you find rats or mice threatening growing crops or other property of which you are the owner or tenant, you may control them using any legal means.

Rats and house mice are not native to North America but traveled along on ships bringing early European settlers. They are among the numerous imports that are considered invasive species.

CONTROL METHODS

To successfully control rats and house mice you must work on three fronts:

- sanitation measures and habitat modification
- building construction and rodent proofing or exclusion
- population control

FIGURE 118.

Roof rats damage oranges while the fruit is still on the tree.

FIGURE 119.

This dying citrus branch has been girdled by roof rat feeding.

Sanitation Measures and Habitat Modification

Good housekeeping within buildings should reduce available shelter and food for rats and house mice. Take special efforts to store food items in a way that makes them inaccessible to rodents. Do not leave dirty dishes in the sink; use tight-fitting lids on garbage receptacles; do not leave pet food out at night. Floors in areas where food is prepared and served should be swept or vacuumed daily, leaving no food particles behind. Sanitation not only reduces available food for rats and mice, it is essential for increased effectiveness of traps or poison baits, as hunger makes them accept the bait more readily. Good sanitation practices are not as effective for mice as they are for rats because mice are small and need less food to survive. Problems associated with house mice in buildings by far outnumber those associated with rats.

Similar measures taken outdoors are commonly referred to as habitat modification, but the objectives are the same—reduce available food and cover. For roof rats in particular, thinning dense shrubs and vines makes the habitat less desirable. Climbing vines such as Algerian or English ivy growing on fences or buildings are very conducive to roof rat infestations and should be removed if possible. Trim trees and tall shrubs away from roof edges so that roof rats cannot move between the two. Palm trees are frequently used for nesting; remove dead fronds to reduce available nest sites.

Neatly stacked, off-the-ground storage of pipes, lumber, firewood, crates, boxes, and garden equipment reduces cover for rats and mice. Pick up and dispose of fallen fruit and refrain from placing food items on the compost pile. Do not leave pet food out overnight. Place garbage in rodent-proof cans with tight-fitting lids. Since rats can survive by feeding on pet feces, pick up and bury or dispose of these on a regular basis. Rats and house mice feed on birdseed; consider discontinuing this practice until the rodents are under control. Even if bird feeders are rodent-proof, there is usually enough spillage on the ground to sustain a rodent population.

Exclusion

The most successful and permanent method of controlling rats and mice in buildings is to make a building rodent-proof. Seal cracks and openings in the foundation and openings for water pipes, power or cable lines, sewer pipes, and air vents. No hole larger than ¼ inch (6.5 mm) should be left unsealed. Make sure that doors fit tightly at the bottom and install special seals and weather stripping where needed. Coarse steel wool, wire screen, and lightweight sheet metal are excellent materials for plugging gaps and holes. Thin wood, plastic sheeting, plastic foam, and other less sturdy materials are likely to be gnawed away. Because rats and mice are excellent climbers, openings above ground level must also be plugged, so pay special attention to broken or unscreened air vents on and at the roofline. Most homes can be made completely rat-proof, but making them mouse-proof is much more difficult.

Garden tool or storage sheds and swimming pool pump enclosures can also be made rodent-proof by closing all entry points. Screen off the open spaces beneath them so that rodents will not have nesting sites. Rodents also nest beneath doghouses, rabbit hutches, and aviaries, taking advantage of the nearby food resources.

Trapping

Under most conditions, trapping is the safest and easiest method for controlling rats and mice in and around homes, garages, and other structures, especially when only a few animals are present. The simple wooden snap trap of appropriate size is the most commonly used kill trap because it is inexpensive and very effective. They are available with regular triggers or with expanded plastic triggers. There are, however, many other types of traps available. Multiple-catch mouse traps can be quite effective but are more expensive. Rat-size multiple-catch traps are available, but they are not nearly as effective as those for mice. Live-catch traps present the problem of dispatching of the animals. Releasing house mice or rats elsewhere is in violation of the Fish and Game Code.

The kind of bait used for the trap is important. Nutmeats and fresh or dried fruit are especially effective for roof rats. Cooked bacon, cheese, and dry cat or dog food make good baits for Norway rats and house mice. Gumdrops, cookies, or chocolate candy can also be used. Try several baits and then pick the most favored for further trapping. Fasten the bait securely to the trigger of the trap with light string, thread, or fine wire so the rodent will spring the trap while attempting to remove the food. Dry dog or cat food pieces can be glued to the trigger with standard white glue. Soft baits such as peanut butter or soft cheese can be used, but rats and mice are frequently able to eat these baits without setting off the trap. Leaving traps baited but unset until the bait has been taken at least once improves success by making the rodents more accustomed to the traps. Set traps so the trigger is sensitive and will spring easily.

The best places to set traps are in secluded areas where rats and mice are likely to travel and seek shelter. Droppings, gnaw marks, and damage indicate the presence of rodents, and areas where this evidence is found are usually good places to set traps. Place traps in natural travel ways, such as along walls, so the rodents pass directly over the trigger of the trap (fig. 120). Traps set along a wall should extend from the wall at a right angle, with the trigger end nearly touching the wall. Traps with expanded plastic triggers or treadles work especially well when set along walls because they can be more easily triggered by the rat or mouse when it steps on the treadle. Traps can also be set on ledges or shelves or fastened with screws or wire to branches, fences, pipes, or beams (figs. 121–122). Trapping in these elevated areas is extremely useful for controlling roof rats. In areas where children, pets, or birds might contact traps, use some kind of a barrier to keep them away or set the trap inside a box with a rodent-size entrance hole (fig. 123).

Use as many traps as is practical so that the trapping time will be short and decisive. A dozen or more traps for a heavily infested home may be necessary. Mice seldom venture far from their shelter and food supply, so

FIGURE 120.

Set traps along walls so rats pass over the treadle. A box or board may be used to guide the rat into the trap.

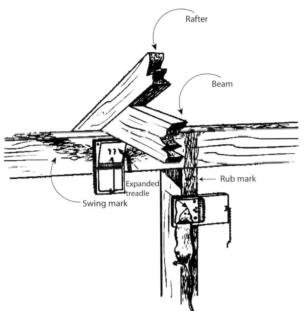

FIGURE 121.

Overhead traps are very effective against roof rats. Purchase traps with an expanded treadle and fasten them to beams or studs using screws or wires so that the treadle is directly in the pathway of the rat.

FIGURE 122.

Set traps on an overhead pipe by drilling a hole in the trap base near the trigger or treadle. Twist a short wire around the pipe and insert a free end up into the hole in the trap. Attach a long, soft wire from the other end of the trap to the pipe. When a rat springs the trap, the rat and trap will fall off the pipe and be held by the long wire, leaving the pipe open for rats to travel to other traps.

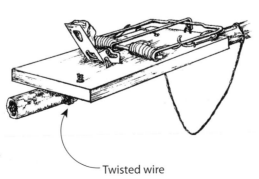

Twisted wire

place traps 10 feet (3 m) apart or less in areas where signs of mice are observed. Rat traps can be placed somewhat farther apart. Dispose of dead rats and mice by burying or placing them in plastic bags in the trash. Do not touch them with your bare hands and wash thoroughly after handling traps.

Glue Boards

An alternative to traps are glue boards, especially for house mice. They work on the same principle as flypaper: when a rat or mouse attempts to cross the glue board, it gets stuck. Place glue boards in secluded areas along walls or in other places where rodents travel. If the rodent travel route includes a place where they jump from one level to another, place the glue board where it is likely to be jumped onto. It is not necessary to bait glue boards. Glue boards tend to lose their effectiveness in dusty areas, and extremes of temperature may affect the tackiness of the adhesive. In many cases, mice and rats trapped on glue boards will not die immediately. If this happens, use a sturdy rod or stick to kill them with a sharp, crushing blow to the base of the skull.

Toxic Bait

If the population of rats or mice in or around a building is high, toxic bait may be needed to achieve adequate and timely control. A number of anticoagulant rodenticides are available for rat and house mice control in and around buildings, including brodifacoum, bromadiolone, chlorophacinone, difethialone, diphacinone, and warfarin. All have the same mode of action, but some may produce somewhat quicker results than others. Generally, the bait must be fed upon for several days, and there is an additional delay of a day or two before death occurs. In case of an accidental ingestion, directions for the physician on the label of all anticoagulant baits list vitamin K₁ as the antidote. The presence of this antidote on the label is a clear indication that the product contains an anticoagulant. These baits are sold under a variety of trade names by many different firms. Anticoagulants are the most common rodent bait used around the home and garden, but other types of bait can also be effective.

Several nonanticoagulant rodenticides are also sold for rat and house mice control in and around buildings. These include bromethalin, cholecalciferol, and zinc phosphide. As a group, these generally give faster results and are less prone to produce secondary poisoning as a result of an animal feeding repeatedly on poisoned rodent carcasses. Of this group, bromethalin and cholecalciferol are the two most common rat and house mice bait products. Zinc phosphide baits are most often used in agricultural situations and may be more difficult to find at your local hardware store or nursery supply. Marketed products for rat and house mice control that are registered by the U.S. EPA must meet stringent efficacy criteria; all are very effective when used as directed. Read and follow baiting directions on the label. Most cases of accidental poisoning occur as a result of failure to follow label instructions. As you would with any poison, take care to ensure the safety of children and pets by preventing their access to the bait.

Although rats and mice are poisoned outdoors, they often die in inaccessible locations within a building, resulting in unpleasant and persistent odors. Rodent-proof nearby buildings before you use toxic baits outside. In fact, because of this potential odor problem, it is rarely recommended to bait rodents within a residence.

Pick up and dispose of dead rodents by burying them or placing them in plastic bags and putting them in the trash (see fig. 1, page 10). Use gloves and wash thoroughly after handling dead rodents, traps, or bait stations. All bait containers should be clearly labeled with appropriate warnings. Store bait in its original container in a locked cabinet or other area inaccessible to children and domestic animals.

Baiting Techniques

For the control of house mice, bait placement is critical. Place baits close to where the mice are living and no farther than 5 to 10 feet (1.5 to 3 m) apart.

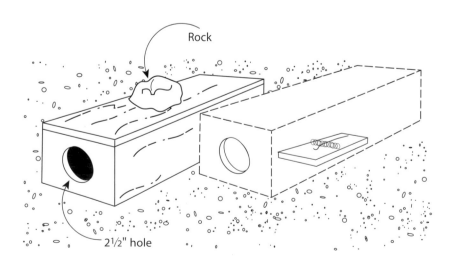

FIGURE 123.

To protect nontarget animals, set rat traps in a wooden box and anchor the box with a heavy weight.

FIGURE 124.

Commercial tamper-resistant rat bait station. Place stations along travel ways of Norway rats and house mice.

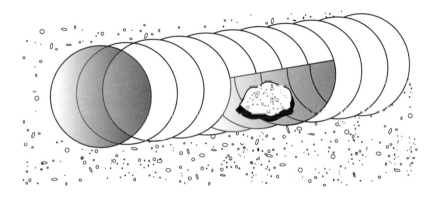

FIGURE 125.

Corrugated 4-inch drain tubing can be made into rat bait stations. Place the bait in the center of the stations. The corrugations help prevent loose bait from being spilled as the animals move in and out.

For rats, place all baits in travel ways or near rat burrows and harborage. Do not expect rats to go out of their way to find the bait. It is a good idea to place baits under cover so the rats will feel secure while feeding. Bait placements for Norway rats are generally not effective for roof rats because the two species nest and find shelter in different areas. Place baits for roof rats in elevated locations such as in the crotch of a tree, on the top of a fence, or high in a vine. If bait is placed above ground level, make sure that the bait

or bait station is securely fastened so that it will not fall to the ground where children or pets may find it.

Rats and mice must feed on most anticoagulant baits several times to be effective, although some single-feeding anticoagulant and nonanticoagulant baits are available. For the best results, the bait must be available for 5 or more days unless otherwise specified on the product label. If bait becomes moldy or insect-infested, replace it and continue baiting until feeding stops. Toxic baits are available in meal, whole grain, and pelleted or extruded forms. In addition, they are marketed in small to large blocks. These bait blocks consist of a combination of rodenticide-treated grains embedded in paraffin or other waxes. Bait blocks have become very popular and make bait application easier. In addition, rats and mice are less apt to scatter or cache bait presented in this form. When using bait blocks, make sure they are not accessible to children or pets.

Bait Stations

Bait stations or boxes limit poison bait exposure and accessibility to rats and mice, providing a safeguard for children, pets, and other animals. The stations should be large enough to accommodate several rats or mice at a time and should contain either a self-feeding hopper or bait compartment for holding the bait. Each station should have at least two 1-inch (2.5-cm) openings for mice or two 2½-inch (6.5-cm) openings for rats. Commercial tamper-resistant stations are available in sizes for house mice or rats and are generally made of sturdy plastic or metal (fig. 124). Some people prefer to construct their own bait boxes; these are usually made of wood, are hinged for ease of access, and have a clasp for locking to make them tamper-resistant. Corrugated 4-inch drainage tubing can also be made into bait stations (fig. 125).

All bait stations should be clearly labeled with the appropriate warnings.

To ensure that a bait station used indoors is truly tamper-resistant, it must be secured to the wall, floor, rafter, or some other part of the structure so that it cannot be tipped over, spilling the bait. If used outdoors, away from a building, it must be securely staked to the ground or well anchored in a tree. When used outdoors, a bait station provides the additional advantage of keeping bait dry in inclement weather as well as safeguarding nontarget animals. For reasons of safety alone, the use of bait stations is highly recommended. When using bait stations, follow the rodenticide label carefully.

As with traps, bait stations must be placed where rodent sign is evident. Indoors, place them along walls, on rafters, within a cupboard, and so on. However, indoor baiting is not recommended because the rodent may die in an inaccessible place, creating an unpleasant odor. For roof rats outdoors, place stations in trees, on rooftops, on fences, or on other elevated spots, if allowed on the label. For Norway rats, place stations on travelways or near burrows or any other site showing evidence of their presence. Follow label instructions carefully when placing and baiting stations.

Other Control Methods

Rats and mice are cautious animals, easily frightened by unfamiliar or strange noises. However, they quickly become accustomed to repeated noises, including sounds emitted by high-frequency devices promoted for control in home and garden situations. Frightening devices in general have not been proved to be effective for rat and house mice control. Rats and mice have an initial aversion to some odors and tastes, but no repellents have been found to repel them for more than a very short time, if at all.

Wild predators such as owls, foxes, skunks, raccoons, opossums, and snakes do feed on rats and house mice, but, because of the reproductive potential of rodents, the predators, in most cases, are unable to keep rat and mice numbers below damaging levels.

Some cats and dogs are good rat and mice catchers, but a sufficient number of rodents are clever enough to escape and thrive in their presence. In fact, according to some studies, people who keep pet cats, and especially dogs, are more apt to have rodent infestations than those who do not, probably because the pet food is available to the rats or mice.

MONITORING GUIDELINES

Because rats and mice are essentially nocturnal, they may go undetected outdoors for some time. Indoors their sign becomes very evident. If roof rats invade the attic, you will generally hear them running about just after dark; this may be your first clue. When moving your woodpile or other materials, be alert for rodent nests or leftover signs of feeding activity, such as nut shells, fruit pits, empty snail shells, etc. Rodent droppings are also good indicators that rats or mice are present. Pet food bowls found empty in the morning when the pet has not yet fed may be another indication of the presence of rodents. Rats and mice have a tendency to seek warmer quarters in the fall and winter, so this is when they often move indoors. Experience has shown that it is less time-consuming to control rats and house mice as soon as they are detected rather than waiting for the population to grow, and fewer traps or less bait will be required if control is started early.

SKUNKS

Two species of skunks inhabit California: the more common striped skunk (*Mephitis mephitis*) and the rarer spotted skunk (*Spilogale gracilis*). Both are members of the weasel family (Mustelidae) and are equipped with a powerful and protective scent gland that can spray a potent and pungent liquid as far as 10 feet (3 m). The secretion is acrid enough to cause nausea and can produce severe burning and temporary blindness if it strikes the eyes. The spotted skunk is fewer in number, much less tolerant of human activity, and less apt to become a problem in California.

The striped skunk is about the size of an adult house cat, 2 to 3 feet (0.6 to 0.9 m) long including the tail and weighing 10 to 15 pounds (4.5 to 6.8 kg), with the familiar mostly black fur and white coloring on top of the head and neck (fig. 126). In most animals the white extends down along the back, usually separating into two white stripes. Spotted skunks are black with white spots or short streaks of white. They are smaller than striped skunks, about half the size of a house cat.

Skunks are nocturnal, hunting for insects, grubs, small rodents, snakes, frogs, mushrooms, berries and fruit, pet food, bird food, and garbage in urban and suburban areas. Skunks have a high preference for eggs and, as a result, are serious

FIGURE 126.

Striped skunk. Skunks found wandering about during the daylight may have rabies.

FIGURE 127.

Skunks sometimes dig under tool sheds and other buildings to create space for dens.

FIGURE 128.

At night, skunks seek out food scraps near garbage cans.

predators of ground-nesting birds.

Skunks usually breed during February and March, with litters born about 9 weeks later. Litters range from 4 to 6 kits. In a few months the kits will be seen following their mother as she makes her nightly rounds in search of food. Skunks do not hibernate, but in regions of colder weather, females may assemble in communal dens during the winter.

Skunks often den in burrows but prefer to do as little digging as possible. They will use and, if necessary, enlarge an abandoned burrow dug by a ground squirrel, fox, or coyote. If dens are scarce they readily use brush piles, hollow logs, and culverts. In urban settings, they den under decks, porches, or beneath buildings when accessible (fig. 127).

Skunks are a primary carrier of rabies in California, so when they take up residence in an urban or suburban area there is cause for concern. Rabies is a viral disease transmitted by the bite of an infected animal. Skunks are also carriers of other diseases including leptospirosis, listeriosis, canine distemper, canine hepatitis, Q-fever, tularemia, and trypanosoma (see table 1).

Skunks are attracted to residential areas by the availability of food, water, and shelter (fig. 128). They become a nuisance when they live under open porches, decks, and garden sheds or, if access is possible, beneath a home. Ripening berries and fallen fruit are a favorite food of skunks. Many garden problems are caused by their digging activities while in search of grubs and other insects. In lawns they often dig small pits or cone-shaped depressions ranging from 3 to 5 inches (7.5 to 12.5 cm) across in search of food items. As with raccoons, skunks may also roll back sections of newly laid sod in searching for insects.

LEGAL RESTRAINTS OF CONTROL

The California Fish and Game Code classifies skunks as nongame mammals. The owner or tenant of the premises may take at any time and in any legal manner nongame mammals injuring or threatening property. Fish and Game regulations prohibit the relocation of skunks and other wildlife without written permission of the DFG. The prevalence of rabies in the skunk population is one of several major reasons for denying relocation. For further information on the legal status of skunks, contact the DFG.

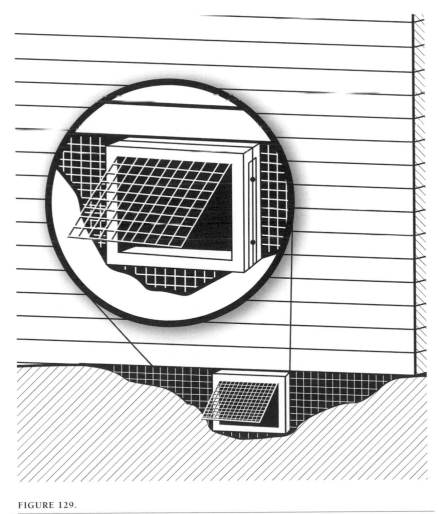

FIGURE 129.

One-way hinged door for preventing skunks or opossums from returning to a den beneath a building.

CONTROL METHODS

Because rabies is endemic in the skunk population, some city and county health departments assist in their control by providing trappers to remove them from residential areas. Skunks' habit of spraying their musk-laden secretion is sufficient to make them unwelcome visitors, especially in close proximity to homes. Control methods focus on making the garden, yard, and residence less attractive to skunks; trapping can be used if these methods are not sufficient.

Habitat Control

Cut back overgrown shrubbery and tightly stack firewood to reduce potential den sites. Remove and dispose of fallen fruit. Garbage cans should have tight-fitting lids. Do not place food items or table scraps in your compost bin. Food placed outdoors for pets should be removed by nightfall.

Exclusion

As with many other vertebrate pests, the best solution to skunk problems beneath porches or buildings is to screen or block them out. Close off all potential entrances or openings under houses, garden sheds, mobile homes, porches, and decks with ¼-inch (6.5-mm) mesh hardware cloth. The advantage of using the small mesh is that it will also exclude rats and house mice if it is installed correctly. Skunks will work hard to get into a desirable denning space, so make sure that the screen fits tightly. If there is soil underneath the screen, bury the screen 6 inches (15 cm) deep to make a good seal.

Once skunks have made their home beneath a building, exclusion is more difficult because you must make sure the animals have left before blocking the opening. Sprinkle a smooth layer of flour about ⅛ inch (3 mm) thick in front of the point of entrance to form a tracking patch. Examine the tracking patch soon after dark; the presence of footprints indicates that the animal has left and the opening can be closed. The problem is compounded if the den contains young skunks. If you are unsure of the number of skunks beneath a building, install a one-way outward swinging gate made from ½-inch (12.5-mm) mesh hardware cloth. Hinge the gate at the top and leave it loose on the other three sides. Make the gate larger than the opening so that it can only swing outward (fig. 129). If the kits are not yet mobile, this gate will be ineffective, and they may have to be removed by other means. Placing one or more floodlights beneath the building opposite the skunk's entry point often helps drive them out of a location. A well-lit area is not conducive to denning.

Trapping

Skunks can be trapped with an enclosed cage-type live-catch trap. Plastic box traps are superior to wire traps because they are completely enclosed, reducing the risk of getting sprayed while removing the trapped animal from the site. Individuals who have no experience in trapping skunks should hire a professional wildlife control operator. They have the experience and all the necessary equipment to trap and dispatch the animal and are also much less apt to be sprayed, an event to be avoided if at all possible. Skunks cannot be relocated without a permit, and it is unlikely that DFG would issue one because of the potential for spreading rabies.

Other Control Methods

Commercial products are available for repelling skunks, but unfortunately they are not very effective. The odor of mothballs or ordinary household ammonia has been used as a home remedy repellent, with some success reported in driving skunks from beneath buildings.

Another suggested method of skunk control is to spray your lawn with an appropriate insecticide to control grubs and other insects, reducing the food for skunks and discouraging them from further digging. If your lawn is infested with insects or grubs, contact your local University of California Cooperative Extension office or garden supply store for information on how to control these pests.

Burrow fumigants, such as gas or smoke cartridges used on ground squirrels, may be used in rural areas if the burrows used by skunks can be located and are not under or near buildings and this use is allowed on the product label. Fumigants are not generally recommended for use in residential areas because of the risk of fire and of gas penetrating into buildings. To use them, ignite the cartridges and push them into the skunk's burrow. Seal off the burrow with soil and pack it tightly to prevent the toxic and asphyxiating smoke from escaping. Follow the product instructions carefully.

In rural areas where it is safe to do so, skunks may be spotlighted at night and shot. Since they may spray in the process, be selective in the location chosen for this control method.

ODOR REMOVAL

The chemical neutroleum-alpha, or products that contain this ingredient, is probably the best neutralizer of the unpleasant skunk scent, but this material is often not readily available. Other products are sold for neutralizing or masking skunk odor. If you cannot find odor removal products easily, call a professional wildlife control operator to see if they can recommend a source. If your dog or cat has been sprayed by a skunk, call your veterinarian to determine current recommendations for washing the animal to get rid of skunk odor. A home remedy formulation that has been reported to be effective is

- 1 quart (0.9 l) 3% hydrogen peroxide
- ¼ cup (60 ml) baking soda
- 1 teaspoon (5 ml) liquid soap

Once the hydrogen peroxide is mixed with the baking soda, the mixture generates oxygen and becomes unstable and cannot be bottled or stored. Applying this mixture leads to oxidation, which apparently changes the chemical composition of skunk scent so that it no longer smells. When the fresh mixture is applied to items contaminated by skunk odor, the smell diminishes quickly. Any leftover mixture should be diluted several times with water and poured down the drain.

SKUNK BITES

Rabies is an infectious disease caused by a virus (rhabdovirus) found in the saliva of infected animals. The disease affects only mammals and is generally transmitted by a bite. With the exception of bats, the disease is almost always fatal to animals. People can survive the bite of a rabid animal but only if medical attention is received in time. A physician should attend to **ALL** skunk bites, and the local health department should be notified of the incident.

Skunks that seem tame or listless and wander about during daylight hours should be treated with great caution, since this behavior is symptomatic of rabies. Also, if they exhibit no fear of people or pets and show some aggressive behavior, the chances are quite high that they are rabid.

If you live in an area where there are skunks, be sure your dogs and cats are routinely vaccinated against rabies. Some dogs will confront skunks whenever they get an opportunity, even though they suffer when they get sprayed.

MONITORING GUIDELINES

Because skunks are active at night, many people never see them as they travel through their neighborhoods or yards. Barking dogs may be the first apparent clue. A confrontation between a skunk and a dog provides positive evidence of a skunk problem. If skunks travel through your yard or garden repeatedly, you should be able to detect a faint skunk odor, even if a skunk has not sprayed. As with raccoons, an occasional visit by a skunk or a family of skunks may not present cause for concern, but if these visits become commonplace, action is probably warranted. During the breeding season males frequently spray when fighting over females. The presence of skunk odor in late winter is a signal to keep an eye out for the presence of skunks. At this time, appropriate measures may be necessary to deny pregnant females access to potential nesting sites underneath buildings.

FIGURE 130.

Eastern fox squirrel, also referred to as the red fox squirrel.

TREE SQUIRRELS

Four species of tree squirrels are found in California, excluding the small nocturnal flying squirrel (*Glaucomys volans*), which is not considered a pest: eastern fox squirrel (*Sciurus niger*) (fig. 130), eastern gray squirrel (*S. carolinensis*) (fig. 131), western gray squirrel (*S. griseus*), and Douglas squirrel (*Tamiasciurus douglasii*). Of the four, western gray and Douglas are native and the other two were introduced from the eastern part of the United States. Tree squirrels range from 12 to 29 inches (30.5 to 73.5 cm) long, including the bushy tail. They are somewhat larger than ground squirrels, whom they otherwise resemble. Unlike ground squirrels, tree squirrels tend to climb trees or other objects to escape danger.

In their natural habitats all four species eat a variety of foods, including fungi, insects, bird eggs, young birds, pine nuts, and acorns, along with a wide range of other seeds. Tree squirrels sometimes cause damage around homes and gardens where they feed on immature and mature almonds, English and black walnuts, oranges, avocados, apples, apricots, and a variety of other items. During ground foraging they may feed on strawberries, tomatoes, corn, and other crops. They also have a habit, principally in the fall, of digging holes in garden soil or in turf, where they bury nuts, acorns, or other seeds. This caching of food, which they may not ever retrieve, raises havoc in the garden and tears up a well-groomed lawn. They sometimes gnaw on telephone cables and may chew into wooden

FIGURE 131.

Eastern gray squirrel in Golden Gate Park, San Francisco.

FIGURE 132.

Western gray squirrel damage to a cedar tree.

buildings or invade attics through gaps or broken vent screens. Tree squirrels carry diseases that are transmissible to people and are frequently infested with fleas, mites, and other ectoparasites (see table 1).

Tree squirrels are active during the day and are frequently seen in trees, running on utility lines, and foraging on the ground. They are easily distinguished from ground squirrels and chipmunks by their long bushy tails and lack of flecklike spots or stripes, and by the fact that they escape danger by climbing trees and other structures. All are chiefly arboreal, although the eastern fox and western gray squirrels spend considerable time foraging on the ground. Tree squirrels do not hibernate and are active year round. They are most active in early morning and late afternoon.

The eastern fox squirrel, also called the fox, red, or red fox squirrel, was introduced from the eastern United States and is well established in most major cities of California. Some people enjoy watching them and have transported them from place to place. In some cities they have moved outward into agricultural land, especially in the southern part of the state, where they have become a pest of commercial crops. The eastern gray squirrel was introduced from the eastern United States into Golden Gate Park in San Francisco. It has become established in areas of Calaveras and San Joaquin Counties and may be expanding its range.

The western grey squirrel, native to California, is found throughout much of the state, primarily in oak woodlands of the Sierra foothills and valleys and in pine-oak forests, where they feed on a variety of seeds, fungi, and other plant materials . They often strip bark in order to access and feed on the cambium layer, injuring trees (fig. 132). The native Douglas squirrel, sometimes called the chickaree, is found mostly in conifer-forested regions of the north coastal area and in the Sierra Nevada. Because of the habitat in which they thrive, these two native tree squirrels are not usually pests, except for the damage they can do in forest regeneration projects. They may, however, become pests in rural homes and gardens in their habitat.

Of the four tree squirrels, the eastern fox squirrel is by far the most serious pest to homes and gardens in urban and suburban situations in California. This squirrel can be differentiated from the others by its brownish red-orange fur, which is the color phase commonly seen in California.

Tree squirrels nest in tree cavities, enlarged woodpecker holes, or high in a tree in a spherical nest they construct of twigs, leaves, and shredded bark. They breed in the late winter or in the spring and, depending on the species, produce 1 or 2 litters per year of 3 to 5 young. For those producing 2 litters, the breeding period is extended.

LEGAL RESTRAINTS OF CONTROL

Tree squirrels are classified as game mammals by the Fish and Game Code and can be taken (killed) only as provided by hunting regulations. However, fox squirrels that are found to be injuring growing crops or other property may be taken at any time and in any legal manner by the owner or tenant of the premises. Any owner or tenant of land or property that is being damaged or destroyed or is in danger of being damaged or destroyed by gray squirrels may apply to the DFG for a permit to control such squirrels. The DFG, upon receipt of satisfactory evidence of actual or immediately threatened damage or destruction, may issue a revocable permit for the taking and disposition of such squirrels. When a permit to trap the gray squirrel is issued, the DFG may designate the type of trap to be used and may also require that squirrels be released in parks or other nonagricultural areas. It is not legal to use poison baits to kill tree squirrels in California.

FIGURE 133.

Tree squirrels are excellent jumpers and can leap several feet from trees to rooftops. When possible, keep branches pruned away from roofs.

CONTROL METHODS

In urban and suburban areas tree squirrels are difficult to control because of their great mobility and the fact that many people feed and provide nest boxes for squirrels in order to encourage their presence. It is relatively easy to keep squirrels out of buildings, but keeping them out of a yard or garden is a continuous challenge.

Habitat Modification

Trees that overhang roofs or are close to telephone lines should be cut back to slow the movement of squirrels about the yard (fig. 133). Anything that can be done to make a garden less attractive to squirrels will be helpful.

Exclusion

Screening or blocking all potential entrance sites, including small gaps under the eaves, overlapping roof sections, knotholes, and so on, can deny tree squirrels access to buildings. They frequently find entrances at the height of overhead telephone lines, power lines, and fence tops. When they find even a small opening, they enlarge it by gnawing. In the absence of an obvious entrance, they can gnaw through wood to create an entrance into an attic. Sheet metal or ¼-inch (6.5 mm) wire hardware cloth are suitable materials for closing entrances. When closing entry routes, make sure you have not screened an animal inside the building. One way to test whether any squirrels are left is to plug the entrance with a loose wad of newspaper; if any remain inside they will remove the plug to get out.

It is virtually impossible to keep tree squirrels out of fruit or nut trees because of their superb climbing and jumping ability. If there are other unprotected fruit or nut trees available to the squirrels, you can protect the crop of a single tree by netting it as you would to exclude depredating birds. Although squirrels can easily gnaw

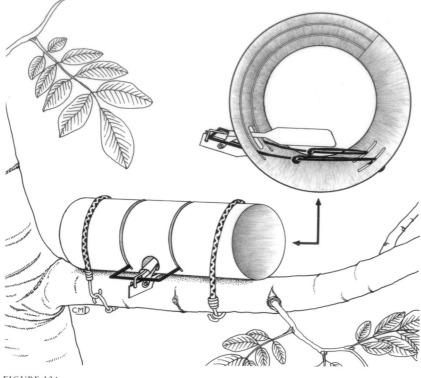

FIGURE 134.

Tube-type or tunnel-type traps effectively trap tree squirrels. These traps are best used in trees frequented by squirrels.

through plastic netting, they may not persist if sufficient alternative food is readily available.

Squirrels can be prevented from digging up newly seeded vegetables and bulb plants by covering rows with poultry wire. Strawberries and tomatoes can also be protected with cagelike free-standing covers made of 1-inch-hexagon (2.5-cm) poultry wire.

If squirrels are present around bird feeders, they can usually reach them and steal the food. Numerous devices and methods are commercially available from specialty catalogs for physically excluding tree squirrels from feeders; some of these work better than others. Tree squirrels are amazingly clever and agile, and it is difficult to exclude them with barriers.

Trapping

Several types of kill traps can be used in taking tree squirrels, but they must be set in a way that will not accidentally trap nontarget

animals, including pets. This can be accomplished by placing the trap in a tree or on a rooftop or inside a box or wire cage with entrances no larger than 3 inches (7.5 cm) in diameter. Only eastern fox squirrels can be killed without a hunting license or permit.

All-metal tunnel or tube-type traps are becoming more popular for killing eastern fox tree squirrels (fig. 134). These devices offer good protection to larger nontarget animals and keep the trapped animal partially out of sight. The Conibear 110 or 120 trap is also an effective tree squirrel trap when set inside a trap box with the bait placed behind the trap (fig. 135). Several choker-type box traps are sold for taking tree squirrels. They look similar to those used for trapping pocket gophers except that the triggers are often reversed so that the bait must be pulled to activate instead of pushed, as is the case with pocket gopher traps. In fact, certain wooden choker-type gopher traps can be modified to make a tree squirrel trap. To modify a gopher trap, lengthen the trigger slot with a rattail file so the trigger can swing unhindered and the squirrel can pass beneath the unset trap. Remove the back and replace with ¼-inch (6.5-mm) hardware cloth, which allows the squirrels to see the bait from both ends but prevents access without passing through the trap. For a dual trap assembly, place two box traps back to back and secure them to a board (fig. 136).

Before placing traps, determine the squirrels' travel routes and place traps in them or as close to them as possible. Trees and rooftops are often good locations. Secure the traps so that they cannot be easily dislodged. Anchor them with a wire or light chain to prevent a predator from carrying the trap and the catch away. Bait the traps but do not set them for several days, allowing the squirrels to steal the bait and become accustomed to the trap.

Once the bait is being taken, set the traps and rebait. Use rubber or plastic gloves when handling dead squirrels. Place them in a plastic bag and seal to confine any ectoparasites. The carcasses can then be discarded in a garbage can.

Sometimes ordinary snap-type rat traps are suggested for tree squirrels, but these are often not powerful enough to kill mature squirrels and should not be used. Kill traps are available for squirrel-sized animals, but these may have to be ordered from a trapper supply firm.

Live-catch cage traps are also available, but once caught the squirrel must be disposed of, presenting a problem for some. Releasing a fox squirrel elsewhere is illegal. Considering this problem, live-catch traps are not recommended. A kill trap is usually the most effective way to thin out the population, but new squirrels will move in to fill the void. Trapping usually must be ongoing once the neighborhood is populated with tree squirrels.

Other Control Methods

Although chemical repellents are registered for discouraging tree squirrels from entering an area, their effectiveness is questionable. Repellents may be added to birdseed that are said to prevent squirrels from feeding on the seeds, but these too have shown little promise.

Tree squirrels quickly become habituated to visual or aural frightening devices and pay little attention to them after a couple of days. A number of these devices are on the market, and none have proved to be very effective.

Where shooting is allowed, the eastern fox tree squirrel can be killed at close range with a pellet gun. Check with local authorities to determine if this method is legal in your area.

Tree squirrels are quick to escape when pursued by predators. Dogs that have full run of a yard may keep squirrels at bay. Predators in urban and suburban areas generally have little effect on tree squirrel populations.

MONITORING GUIDELINES

Tree squirrels are fairly easy to detect because they are active during daylight hours and are highly visible. If tree squirrels visit your garden or yard on a regular basis, it is likely that they will cause damage at certain stages of crop development, particularly in fruit and nut crops. If you see squirrels in your trees, take preventive action such as exclusion or habitat modification. Squirrels can strip a fruit or nut tree of its crop in a short time.

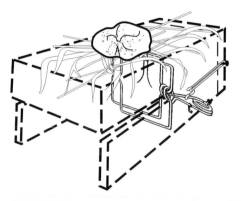

FIGURE 135.

Body-grip Conibear trap in set position inside a long trap box.

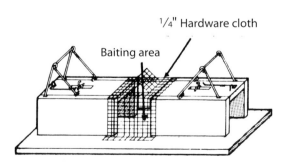

FIGURE 136.

Dual trap assembly using two box-type gopher traps works well for tree squirrels.

Reptiles

FIGURE 137.

Gopher snake devouring a pocket gopher.

California is home to many species of reptiles, including turtles, lizards, and snakes. Turtles are not considered pests, and many are protected as threatened or endangered species. While lizards may sometimes enter dwellings and other structures and be considered pests, they seldom pose major problems. The primary pest reptiles in California are snakes.

Many different species of snakes inhabit the state, and most are harmless to humans (fig. 137). Because they are poisonous, rattlesnakes as a group seem to receive the most attention. All snakes play a role in the ecosystem and should be left alone, except when they pose an immediate danger to people, pets, or livestock.

RATTLESNAKES

The rattlesnake, a member of the pit viper family (Crotalinae), is the only venomous snake native to California. Six species are found in various areas of the state, from below sea level to about 11,000 feet (3,350 m). Adult rattlesnakes can approach 6 feet (1.8 m) in length and 3½ inches (7.5 cm) in diameter (fig. 138). They are an important part of the ecosystem, preying on rodents, birds, and other small animals and in turn being preyed upon, especially by certain birds.

Rattlesnakes have a distinct triangular head, which is a key characteristic in their identification. Nonpoisonous snakes in California do not have this obvious characteristic (fig. 139). A less reliable identifying feature is the rattle. The rattle, on the end of the tail, is composed of interlocking horny segments. Young rattlesnakes are born with a small rattle, or button. A new segment is formed each time the skin is shed, which may occur several times each year. The terminal segments often break off as a snake ages, so the size of the rattle is not a good indicator of age. Also, because they can be broken off, the lack of a rattle does not mean the snake is not a rattlesnake. Some nonpoisonous snakes have a similar coloration as rattlesnakes. The diamond-shaped head is the characteristic that most readily signifies a rattlesnake in California.

The largest and most common rattlesnake in California is the western diamondback *(Crotalus atrox),* which is found primarily in Imperial, Riverside, and San Bernardino Counties from sea level to 7,000 feet (2,130 m) (fig. 140). It is probably the most dangerous rattlesnake in California because of its size and

FIGURE 138.

The rattlesnake is the only native poisonous snake found in California and when seen should be treated with considerable caution. They sometimes rattle their tails when disturbed.

aggressive disposition. The Western rattlesnake (*C. viridis*) is common throughout much of California. It is not found in true desert regions or in areas of the Central Valley where irrigated agriculture has eliminated its habitat. It is generally recognized as comprising three subspecies, Northern Pacific, Southern Pacific, and Great Basin.

The sidewinder (*C. cerastes*), the smallest rattlesnake in the state, is so named because of its peculiar method of sideways locomotion. It is sometimes called the horned rattler because of the hornlike scales above its eyes. Sidewinders are most commonly found in sandy desert areas from below sea level to 6,000 feet (1,820 m). The Mojave rattlesnake (*C. scutulatus*) ranges in the desert and foothills of southeastern California from sea level to high elevations. Speckled rattlesnakes (*C. mitchellii*) are found throughout Baja California and up the coast approximately to Los Angeles, overlapping with the red diamond rattlesnake (*C. ruber*) in most of this area. It also overlaps much of the sidewinder's range in the southeast desert area. The red diamond rattlesnake is found in Baja California and in southwestern California below Los Angeles.

Most rattlesnakes forage for prey in or near brush, areas of tall grass, rock outcrops, rodent burrows, around and under surface objects, and sometimes in the open. Adults eat live prey,

primarily rodents; the young take mostly lizards and young rodents. To catch their prey, rattlesnakes wait until the animal is near. The snake strikes with two large fangs that inject venom. This subdues the prey, which the snake then swallows whole. Rattlesnakes sometimes feed on carrion if no other food is available.

When inactive, most rattlesnakes seek cover in crevices of rocks, under surface objects, beneath dense vegetation, and in rodent burrows. In some areas, rattlesnakes hibernate for several months in crevices in rock accumulations. Unlike most reptiles, rattlesnakes give birth to live young. Young snakes require protection and are likely to be born in abandoned rodent burrows, rock crevices, or in other secluded places.

Rattlesnakes are included in the pit viper family because they have small pits on each side of the head between the eye and nostril (see fig. 139). These pits are temperature-sensitive organs that assist the snake in finding prey, even in total darkness. The nostrils and tongue also detect the odors of prey. Rattlesnakes have the most highly developed venom delivery system of all snakes. Venom is produced in glands behind the eyes and flows through ducts to the hollow fangs. Normally the fangs fold back against the roof of the mouth, but when the snake strikes, the fangs pivot forward to inject venom. The snake can control the amount of venom ejected from either or both

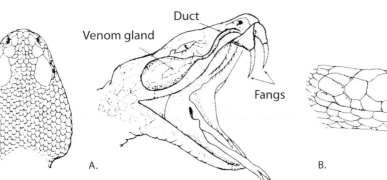

FIGURE 139.

A: Rattlesnake head showing characteristic triangular shape. B: Rattlesnake venom injection organs. C. Pit viper head showing the elliptical pupil and location of the loreal pit.

Duct

Venom gland

Fangs

Elliptical eye pupil

Nostril

Loreal pit

A.

B.

C.

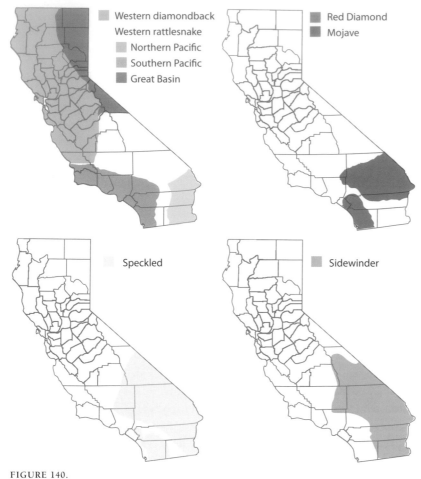

Western diamondback
Western rattlesnake
    Northern Pacific
    Southern Pacific
    Great Basin

Red Diamond
Mojave

Speckled

Sidewinder

FIGURE 140.

California rattlesnakes and their ranges.

in rock crevices, under logs, in heavy brush, or in other areas where they are protected, including tall grass. They can also be found on roads, paths, and other areas where cover is limited. Be careful when moving brush, wood, logs, or other debris. In rattlesnake country, be alert when kneeling down to work in the garden and watch where you step. Since rattlesnakes are often well camouflaged and wait quietly for prey, they can be difficult to see. In the wild, rattlesnakes should be left alone, as they present little potential hazard. Rattlesnakes around the home or garden are not acceptable to most people. Fortunately, there are ways to minimize the potential hazards.

LEGAL RESTRAINTS OF CONTROL

The 6 species of rattlesnakes found in California are not considered endangered or threatened. California Department of Fish and Game Regulations classifies rattlesnakes as native reptiles. California residents can take rattlesnakes on private lands in any legal manner without a license or permit.

CONTROL METHODS

Rattlesnakes add to our wildlife diversity and are important members of our ecosystem, and they should be left alone whenever possible, especially in wildland areas. Nonpoisonous snakes should be left alone wherever they are found. Because of the danger rattlesnakes pose to people, pets, and domestic animals, it can be necessary to exclude or remove them from around homes and gardens.

Habitat Modification

One of the best ways to discourage rattlesnakes around gardens and homes is to remove suitable hiding places. Heavy brush, tall grass, rocks, logs, rotten stumps, lumber piles, and other places of cover should be cleaned

fangs. Even after its death, a rattlesnake can still, by reflex action, inject venom for an hour or more. Caution is therefore advised when handling what appears to be a dead snake.

About 800 rattlesnake bites are reported annually in the United States. While seldom fatal, bites are extremely painful and can lead to severe medical trauma. Those who enjoy hiking should determine whether rattlesnakes are found in the area and under what conditions they might be encountered. The range maps provide a general indication of where rattlesnakes occur in California. However, rattlesnakes may be very sparse or nonexistent in some parts of their range, and they can sometimes be found outside their normal range, transported there by humans or natural mechanisms such as flowing water. If rattlesnakes are in the area, they will most likely be hidden up. Keep weeds mowed close to the ground or remove them. Since snakes often come to an area in search of prey, eliminating rodent populations, especially ground squirrels, meadow voles, deer mice, rats, and house mice, is an important step in modifying the habitat to make it less attractive for snakes. Rattlesnakes cannot dig burrows but frequently use those dug by rodents. After controlling the rodents, fill in all the burrows with soil or sod and pack down firmly.

Exclusion

Rattlesnakes may seek refuge beneath buildings. Where there is a gap or opening, they will enter and inhabit a building, just as do house mice. Sealing all cracks and other openings greater than ¼ inch (6.5 mm) can prevent this. Gaps beneath garage

Rattlesnake Safety

In case of a snakebite, what should I do for initial first aid?

Because most of California is rattlesnake country, develop a snakebite emergency plan before you need it. If you are less than 1 hour from the nearest emergency room, initial treatment is relatively simple:

☐ Try to calm the victim.

☐ Gently wash the area with soap and water.

☐ Apply a cold, wet cloth over the bite.

☐ Transport to the nearest emergency facility for further treatment.

What should I NOT do after a snakebite?

☐ DON'T apply a tourniquet.

☐ DON'T pack the bite area in ice.

☐ DON'T cut the wound with a knife or razor.

☐ DON'T use your mouth to suck out the venom.

☐ DON'T let the victim drink alcohol.

☐ DON'T apply electric shock.

What can be done to prevent snakebites?

Hands, feet, and ankles are the most common sites for rattlesnake bites. Using some commonsense rules can prevent most snakebites.

☐ Never go barefoot or wear sandals when walking in the rough. Always wear heavy shoes or hiking boots.

☐ Always stay on paths. Avoid tall grass, weeds, and heavy underbrush where there may be snakes.

☐ Use a walking stick when hiking. If you come across a snake, it may strike the stick instead of you.

☐ Always look for concealed snakes before picking up rocks, sticks, or firewood.

☐ Always check carefully around stumps or logs before sitting.

☐ When climbing, always look before putting your hands in a new location. Snakes can climb walls, trees, and rocks and are frequently found at high altitudes.

☐ Never grab "sticks" or "branches" while swimming. Rattlesnakes are excellent swimmers.

☐ Baby rattlesnakes are poisonous! They can and do bite. Leave them alone.

☐ Never hike alone. Always have a buddy to help in case of an emergency. Learn basic first aid for snakebites.

☐ Don't handle freshly killed snakes. You may still be bitten.

☐ Never tease a snake to see how far it can strike. You can be several feet from the snake and still be within striking distance.

☐ Don't keep rattlesnakes as pets. The majority of rattlesnake bites occur when people tease or play with their "pet" rattlesnakes.

☐ Teach children to respect snakes and to leave snakes alone. Curious children who pick up snakes are frequently bitten.

☐ Always give snakes the right of way!

In case of a snake bite, call the California Poison Control System: 1-800-876-4766 anytime, from anyplace in California.

doors are often large enough to permit snakes to enter, especially young ones. In the summer rattlesnakes may be attracted to cool or damp places, such as beneath buildings and in basements. Access doors on crawl holes should be inspected carefully for breaks or gaps. Use caution if you must crawl under a house or other building. Pump enclosures for hot tubs or swimming pools may provide cover if not well sealed. The dampness associated with ornamental water fountains, pools, and fishponds may also make the surrounding area attractive to snakes.

Fences

Snakes can be excluded from an area by a snake-proof fence. While expensive, this is often necessary for children's play areas. Make gates fit tightly and keep vegetation and debris from collecting around the fence. Snakes can climb accumulated vegetation and gain access to the top of the fence. Check the fence frequently to make sure it has not been damaged in any way.

Repellents

Over the years a number of home remedies have been suggested to repel snakes, such as placing a horsehair rope around your sleeping bag or sprinkling sulfur dust or scattering mothballs around the area to be protected. Unfortunately, none of these work. Despite what you sometimes hear, no plants repel snakes. Currently there is at least one commercially available chemical snake repellent on the market, but it has not been proved sufficiently effective to warrant its recommendation.

Other Control Methods

If left alone, a snake will likely move away from you and on to another area. If necessary, kill rattlesnakes with a shovel or club. Rattlesnakes are capable of striking quickly, so caution

is important. They can also be killed by shooting if it is allowed by local regulation. If you don't want to kill the snake, yet want it removed, call a professional pest or wildlife control operator who specializes in snake removal. The county agricultural commissioner or University of California Cooperative Extension offices may be able to direct you to professionals who remove rattlesnakes. Most rattlesnake bites occur when inexperienced people try to pick up or move a rattlesnake.

Several predators feed on rattlesnakes, including the king snake, which swallows them whole. Unfortunately, the number of rattlers eaten by predators is insignificant in reducing a problem you might encounter around your home or garden

MONITORING GUIDELINES

Rattlesnake detection is difficult because they are not easy to see or to locate in their hiding places. Be alert to their potential presence during the time of year when rattlesnakes are generally active in your region. If rattlesnakes become exceptionally numerous in an area, sightings by neighbors may alert you to expect a problem. Snake populations may fluctuate from year to year; this is thought to be related in part to the availability of prey. Some animals, such as peacocks, turkeys, and dogs, can be good sentinels for detecting rattlesnakes. If your dog behaves in an unusual manner, excessively barking or whining, it would be wise to investigate for the possible presence of a snake. A veterinarian should immediately attend to dogs or domestic animals bitten by a rattlesnake. If you have a snake-proof fence, be sure to check its integrity before snakes become active in the late winter or early spring. Keeping the rodent population in and around your yard under control is an excellent way to discourage snakes of all kinds.

Bibliography

Bjornson, B. F., and C. V. Wright. 1960. Control of domestic rats and mice. Rev. ed. Center for Disease Control, USDHEW, Public Health Service Publication 563.

Brenzel, K. N., ed. 2001. Sunset western garden book. 7th ed. Menlo Park, CA: Sunset Publishing.

Flint, M. L. 2001. IPM in practice: Principles and methods of integrated pest management. Oakland: University of California Division of Agriculture and Natural Resources Publication 3418.

Gorenzel, W. P., and T. P. Salmon. 1997. Controlling urban crow roosts with taped distress calls. Oakland: University of California Division of Agriculture and Natural Resources Publication 21561. Includes tape.

Chapman, J. A., and G. A. Feldhamer, eds. 1982. Wild mammals of North America: Biology, management, economics. Baltimore: Johns Hopkins University Press.

Coey, B., and K. Mayer. 1997. A gardener's guide to preventing deer damage. Sacramento: California Department of Fish and Game.

Conover, M. 2002. Resolving human-wildlife conflicts. Boca Raton, FL: Lewis Publishers.

Corrigan, R. M. 2001. Rodent control: A practical guide for pest management professionals. Cleveland, OH: GIE Media.

Hadidian, J., G. R. Hodge, and J. W. Grandy, eds. 1997. Wild neighbors. Golden, CO: Fulcrum.

Hart, R. M. 1997. Deer proofing your yard and garden. Pownal, VT: Storey Publishing.

————. 1999. Squirrel proofing your home and garden. Pownal, VT: Storey Publishing.

Hygnstrom, S. E., R. M. Timm, and G. E. Larson. 1994. Prevention and control of wildlife damage. Lincoln: University of Nebraska, USDI, and Great Plains Agr. Council Wildlife Committee.

Link, R. 2004. Living with wildlife in the Pacific Northwest. Seattle: University of Washington Press.

O'Connor-Marer, P. J. 2000. The safe and effective use of pesticides. 2nd ed. Oakland: University of California Division of Agriculture and Natural Resources Publication 3324.

————. In press. Residential, industrial, and institutional pest control. 2nd ed. Oakland: University of California Division of Agriculture and Natural Resources Publication 3334

Storer, T. I., and E. W. Jameson Jr. 1965. Control of field rodents on California farms. Oakland: University of California Division of Agricultural Sciences Circular 535.

University of California Statewide Integrated Pest Management Program (UC IPM). Pest notes. Available for free downloading from the UC IPM Web site at http://www.ipm.ucdavis.edu/. Vertebrate pest notes include: California Ground Squirrel, Cliff Swallows, Deer, House Mouse, Lizards, Moles, Opossum, Pocket Gophers, Rabbits, Raccoons, Rats, Rattlesnakes, Skunks, Tree Squirrels, Voles (Meadow Mice), and Woodpeckers.

Glossary

accumulate. To increase in quantity within an area, such as in the soil or tissues of a plant or animal.

active ingredient. Material in a pesticide formulation that destroys the target pest or performs the desired function.

aestivation or estivation. State of dormancy in an animal's activity cycle occurring during summer months.

anticoagulant. A class or group of rodenticides that causes death by preventing normal blood clotting. Examples include warfarin, chlorophacinone, and brodifacoum.

bait. A food or foodlike substance that attracts animals to traps; food treated with a poison to kill a pest species.

bait box. Used interchangeably with "bait station." Small structure in which a rodenticide bait is placed so that the target animal must enter to feed on the bait. Bait boxes exclude animals larger than the target species.

bait station. See **bait box.**

biological control. The action of parasites, predators, pathogens, or competitors in maintaining another organism's density at a lower average population level than would occur in their absence. Biological control may occur naturally in the field or be the result of manipulation or introduction of biological control agents by people.

browsing. To feed on leaves and shoots of plants and trees.

burrow. An underground excavation used for shelter, food storage, and rearing of young; the living space of a subterranean fossorial mammal.

Caution. Signal word used on labels of pesticides having an oral LD_{50} toxicity greater than 500 mg/kg. Indicates the lowest hazard, beneath **Warning** and **Danger.**

colonial nesting. The nesting of many pairs of birds on one building, in one tree, or in one small area.

control. To regulate, restrain, or curb the population of a wildlife species that has become a pest. Sometimes used interchangeably with "management," as in "pest control" or "pest management."

Danger. The signal word used on labels of pesticides in toxicity Category 1, pesticides with an oral LD_{50} less than 50, or a dermal LD_{50} less than 200, or those having specific serious health or environmental hazards. Indicates the highest hazard, above **Warning.**

depredation. Despoiling or plundering of a crop by a pest animal or species.

disease. A condition caused by biotic or abiotic factors that impairs some or all of the normal functions of a living organism.

diurnal. Active mostly during the day.

economic damage. Damage caused by pests to plants, animals, or other items that results in loss of income or a reduction in value.

efficacy. The ability of a pesticide to produce a desired effect on a target organism.

exclusion. Preventing one or more animals or species of animals from entering a building or an area.

exposure. Coming in contact with a pesticide.

food cache. A quantity of food stored by an animal for later use.

forb. Any small broadleaved flowering plant.

frightening device. Device that drives a pest species away from a crop, area, or building by scaring it. Examples are gas cannons, shell crackers, flags, and noisemakers.

fumigant. Substance that produce toxic or suffocating gases, often used to kill burrowing rodents (burrow fumigant).

game mammal. Mammal specified by the California Fish and Game Code to be hunted for food or sport.

glue board. A small cardboard sheet or boxlike apparatus having one or more surfaces coated with a thick sticky paste. These are placed to capture pest insects or small rodents.

habitat modification. Pest management practice of altering the environment in which an animal species is found. In wildlife pest control this is sometimes done to make the habitat less favorable for the species concerned.

hibernation. State of dormancy in an animal's activity cycle generally occurring during winter months.

inhalation. The method of entry of a disease or pesticide through the nose or mouth into the lungs.

integrated pest management (IPM). A pest management program that uses life history information and extensive monitoring to understand a pest and its potential for causing economic damage. Control is achieved through multiple approaches, including prevention, cultural practices, pesticide applications, exclusion, natural enemies, and host resistance. The goal is to achieve long-term suppression of target pests with minimal impact on nontarget organisms and the environment.

introduced species. A species released by humans or human activity in an area where it was not previously found.

invertebrate. An animal having an external skeleton or shell, such as insects, spiders, mites, worms, nematodes, and snails and slugs.

lethal. Capable of causing death.

migratory bird. A bird that makes an annual round trip between two geographic regions.

mode of action. The way a pesticide reacts with a pest organism to destroy it.

monitoring. The process of carefully watching the activities, growth, and development of pest organisms over a period of time, often utilizing very specific procedures.

multiple-catch trap. A trap that captures mice or rats without killing them and that can hold several rodents per setting.

natural control. Regulation or restraint of an animal population in a manner conforming to nature. Examples include predators, diseases, and lack of food or cover.

netting. Installing nets to protect a crop or structure from birds and pest mammals.

nocturnal. Active mostly at night.

nongame mammal. An animal not commonly hunted, as specified in the California Fish and Game Code.

nontarget animal. Animals within a pesticide treatment area that are not intended to be controlled by the pesticide application.

nontarget species. A species that is not the object of the control being applied.

omnivorous. Feeding on animal and vegetable matter; subsisting on a wide variety of foods.

pesticide. Substance or mixture of substances intended for preventing, destroying, repelling, or mitigating any insects, rodents, nematodes, fungi, weeds, or any other forms of life declared to be pests; substance or mixture of substances intended for use as a plant regulator, defoliant, or desiccant.

phytotoxic. Injurious and sometimes lethal to plants.

prebaiting. Applying an untreated (nontoxic) bait to an area or bait station prior to applying toxic bait to condition the pest animal to the bait and location; improves acceptance of the toxic bait and increases kills.

predator. Animal that survives by regularly killing another animal (or insect) for food.

repellent. Nontoxic pesticide that keeps target pests away from a treated item or area.

rodent. Any of an order (Rodentia) of relatively small gnawing mammals, such as mice, squirrels, or gophers, that have in both jaws a single pair of incisors with a chisel-shaped edge. The term also broadly refers to small mammals such as moles and shrews that are not rodents.

rodenticide. Pesticide that controls rats, mice, gophers, squirrels, and other rodents; in the broadest sense, any vertebrate pesticide.

runway. Path that an animal or animals commonly travel over or through.

sanitation. The practice of keeping an indoor or outdoor area clean, limiting or removing food, water, and cover for pests. See **habitat modification.**

single-feeding bait. Toxic bait that kills an animal in one feeding. Death may be delayed for several days.

snap trap. A spring-loaded trap that kills mice, rats, and other small vertebrates.

spot-baiting. Placing bait by hand at selected sites. Sometimes also referred to as spot-treating.

target. A pest that is being controlled.

untreated bait. Bait to which no toxic or repellent substance has been applied. Used for prebaiting.

vertebrates. Animals that have an internal skeleton and segmented spine, such as fish, birds, reptiles, and mammals.

Warning. Signal word used on labels of pesticides that have an oral LD_{50} toxicity from 50 to 500 mg/kg. Indicates an intermediate hazard, falling between **Danger** and **Caution.**

wildlife pest. Any species of wild animal, in any area, that becomes a health hazard, causes economic damage, or is a general nuisance to one or more persons.

Index